BIG
Contacts

BIG Contacts

How small businesses
can harness
the power of
technology
to attract and
retain
more
customers.

BOB WALTON

Advantage.

Published by Advantage, Charleston, South Carolina.
Member of Advantage Media Group.

ADVANTAGE is a registered trademark and the Advantage colophon is a trademark of Advantage Media Group, Inc.

Printed in the United States of America.

ISBN: 978-1-59932-289-6
LCCN: 2011938366

Advantage Media Group is proud to be a part of the Tree Neutral® program. Tree Neutral offsets the number of trees consumed in the production and printing of this book by taking proactive steps such as planting trees in direct proportion to the number of trees used to print books. To learn more about Tree Neutral, please visit www.treeneutral.com. To learn more about Advantage's commitment to being a responsible steward of the environment, please visit www.advantagefamily.com/green

Advantage Media Group is a leading publisher of business, motivation, and self-help authors. Do you have a manuscript or book idea that you would like to have considered for publication? Please visit www.amgbook.com or call 1.866.775.1696

Foreword

To be clear, I know nothing at all about CRM software. Or at least I didn't before I read through the not quite finished version of Bob Walton's new book on the subject. Honestly, I probably would have had to think hard to figure out what "CRM" even stood for. I guess the good news is that I've managed to survive and succeed in business anyway. And now, I know a lot more than I did before I sat down with Bob's book and a good cup of coffee.

In case you also don't know, CRM stands for "Customer Relationship Management." I learned that and a lot more, by reading through *BIG Contacts*. While the specific subject of the book is software, much of what I learned is, not surprisingly, in synch with pretty much everything we do here at Zingerman's.

We've managed to grow from two employees in the original small space in 1982 to having over 500 employees. The Zingerman's Community of Businesses today includes the original Delicatessen, Zingerman's Bakehouse, Roadhouse (a sit down restaurant featuring regional American foods), Zingerman's Mail Order, Zingerman's Candy Manufactory, Zingerman's Coffee Company and Zingerman's Creamery. We also have our own training and consulting business, called ZingTrain in which we teach seminars on our approach to business including work on visioning, leadership, training systems, and, of course, customer service. Service is most certainly at the core of all we do. I've written *Zingerman's Guide to Giving Great Service*, we have two training seminars on the subject, and two training DVDs. From reading Bob's book, it's very evident that *BIG Contacts* takes some very similar approaches; service is woven throughout the book.

That we've been able to do what we do without the benefit of CRM software is I suppose a good thing. We'll do over $40,000,000 in sales this year, so I can't tell you that having CRM software is the single most important thing you'll ever do. But I can tell you that after reading *BIG Contacts*; I'm pretty convinced that we at Zingerman's will be learning more about it in the years to come. Clearly, CRM software helps create a setting that fosters both good service and good sales – two things, to be clear, that our business has been built on.

As little as I knew going in, reading Bob's book made clear to me that bringing in CRM software, setting it up and using it successfully isn't as overwhelming as it might seem to those who – like me – have never used it. The good news too is that most everything Bob's saying is simple, down to earth, learnable, easily applicable and eminently teachable. Quite simply, the book is a quick – page way to work your way into the CRM world without having to spend six years and $60,000 just to get yourself comfortable with the context, and buy a basic conversation on the subject.

When you read the story of Bob Walton, and what he and his company, BigContacts have done, you will likely realize, as I did, that CRM software can be of great help to any of us who are actively growing our organizations with a focus on effective sales and service. While I don't know them well, everything I've read tells me that there's a lot of commonality in our approach to business, to customer service, and community. The truth is that even if you never end up buying CRM software, the book still provides valuable information for small businesses – I picked up ten different service and sales tips that we can, and will, put into practice long before we actually make any significant switch in our software. And, in the bigger picture, I'm sold on the software too.

In a down to earth, accessible, unintimidating, kind of work a day way, Bob makes clear that CRM can help us, and any other organization that's looking to grow through sales and service.

–Ari Weinzweig

Co-founding partner and CEO of Zingerman's community of businesses. Author of many books, the most recently of, *Zingerman's Guide to Good Leading, Part 1*; *A Lapsed Anarchist's Approach to Building a Great Business, Part 2*; and *A Lapsed Anarchist's Approach to Being a Better Leader*, which will be published late in 2011. He's also written Zingerman's Guides to "Better Bacon," "Good Eating" and "Giving Great Service." You can learn more about Zingerman's approach to business at zingtrain.com, or to have some of Zingerman's full flavored foods shipped to you at your home or office, by visiting zingermans.com

Table of Contents

All businesses need customers. They are the fundamental requirement in any industry, no matter what you make or do or how big you are. If you are to survive and thrive over the long run, you must find and keep customers.

That's why it is crucial to understand and master the "customer lifecycle." When you have loyal customers, you reap the benefits of the hard work you invested to win them over. Losing them is expensive – it costs several times more to find and acquire a new customer than it does to retain an existing one – and you can avoid that cost by developing a laser-sharp focus on the three phases of their lifecycle.

Businesses commonly struggle to get over the organizational hump that will allow them to better evaluate, understand and improve their day-to-day processes. And for those that are able to get organized, few effectively harness the power of technology to put tools in place for maximum growth.

This book will help to ensure that your small business is on the right track for consistent and meaningful growth. Here is what you will find on the pages ahead:

1. The three key phases of the customer lifecycle, the challenges that exist in each, and the rewards for getting it right.

2. How you can leverage an important technology known as CRM software to help you manage the entire customer lifecycle.

3. How to evaluate your own business – because after all, you can't improve without measuring your needs. You will learn how to determine your strengths and weaknesses in each phase of the customer lifecycle. Then you will be able to confidently research, review, and choose the best CRM system for your business.

Over the past five years, my company has had the opportunity to assist nearly 10,000 small businesses in implementing Customer Relationship Management or CRM software. As you can imagine, with this number of installations, we have seen just about every level of success and failure in adopting this important platform.

From this experience, we have developed an in-depth knowledge of what works and what doesn't. We have seen trends in what companies do and don't do that will ultimately determine their success in implementing CRM.

Our experience has found that a set of best practices can and should be developed based on the mistakes and successes of your predecessors. A set of best practices that are well-defined and easy to follow can save a business countless hours and a lot of money.

According to a recent Forrester Research report, 47 percent of companies studied said that their CRM implementation failed to meet their expectations. Many companies before you already have paid the price in time and money, so why not take the lessons they learned and save the tuition?

Many books have been written about CRM, but most of them either review specific CRM products, or they go off into the details of the technology. Very few are written in plain English offering tools and insights to guide you in developing a CRM strategy – a strategy that will ensure you make good choices and put the right foundation in place to effectively leverage this technology in your business.

The books that do speak to the strategy and planning side of things are usually directed at larger companies. As with many areas of business, the small business is often under-served.

That reality was the very reason I founded BigContacts, and it is the reason I wrote this book – to give the small-business owner a set of tools that are easy to use and can help ensure success.

I speak to small-business owners every day, and many of them ask the same questions in their quest to implement this software. They know that a good CRM system, properly woven into their business, can have a measurable impact on growth.

So how did I get into this business, and what makes me qualified to pontificate on this subject? Prior to founding BigContacts in 2006, I spent 14 years in the financial services industry. During that time, I grew from a one-man operation to a team of over fifteen who managed money for thousands of affluent clients.

As the business continued to grow, things reached a tipping point: The manual processes that my team had in place could no longer handle the growing demands of our client base. We needed to move beyond an Excel spreadsheet where we kept key client data.

In 1999, when we had just a few team members, we purchased and implemented ACT! to manage client data.

However, when our team branched out into multiple offices, ACT! immediately became ill-equipped in the new environment. ACT! is a PC-based application, and you only have access to your important data if you can bring a laptop with you. That is not so hard to do, but the impossible task was to network the constantly changing data and to allow all team members to gain real-time access to the information.

It was back to the drawing board. The team needed a new platform, and quick! In 2001, I set out to find a Web-based application that could solve the need for real-time access to data from multiple locations. This was an early time in the Web-based market for CRM software. I made the decision to go with a base-line version of Salesforce.com, as it was the only version that would fit within the team's technology budget.

This system was Web-based and solved the team's immediate and pressing need for remote, real-time access to client information. That was the good news. The bad news was that the system proved to be bloated with irrelevant features and was not easy for my team to learn to use.

The team finally learned to use the system and was back on track. After we settled in and began to ramp up with the system, it became apparent to me that the system had some holes that inhibited the full potential for serving clients.

The common thread with ACT! and Salesforce is that they appeared to be written more from an engineer's perspective than from the end user's view. It didn't feel as if the people developing the software really understood what went on out in the trenches.

The more the business grew, the more magnified the mismatch with the true needs of the end user became. There came a point that our team required more features and overall capacity to better manage our growing client base. That's when the shock came. I called to upgrade and learned that moving to the very next level meant a fivefold increase in monthly expenses.

There was no other choice, as the team was heavily invested in the system and needed the added features. I reluctantly upgraded and paid the much larger fee, but this was the beginning of the end for my use of "off-the-shelf" software.

In 2005, I got together with a software developer to discuss building an application designed from the ground up from a real user's perspective. The goal was to build a system that was custom-made to address the needs of a small business – mine.

The system needed to be easy to use to ensure quick adoption and consistent use by all members on the team. It also needed to be robust in its capacity so it could handle over $300 million in assets and 1,100 client households.

After several months, a few thousand man hours, and the help of several developers, we had our own beta system. As our team used the program day to day, we continued to tweak and refine its functionality.

The program worked out so well for us that we decided other small businesses needed to know about this great tool. In 2006, BigContacts was born.

This book culminates nearly two decades of my experience as a small-business owner and my journey to find and ultimately build a CRM system that properly addressed the needs of a small business. My goal with this book is to share with you what I have learned on this journey.

The problem with most of the books like this on the market today is that they talk only about how to use specific CRM programs. And if they are more general in nature, they speak more about what to do after you already have purchased the software. They deal with such aspects as best practices for implementation and user adoption.

Those are great resources, but I believe the real key to success, with such an important and central tool as CRM, is to help a small business evaluate how it currently organizes information about its clients and prospects.

This calls for a close look at the systems such businesses use to track work flow so they can consistently deliver on their promises to both clients and prospects. To maximize return on investment, a business must follow an important set of steps – a process – prior to purchasing, implementing, or learning to use a system.

BIG Contacts will help you develop the necessary planning and strategy on the front end so that you are better equipped to navigate through the confusion, make the right decisions, implement the best practices, and get all you can out of this very important software.

The planning part of any business isn't always the most exciting thing to do, but without this very important step on the front end, the best technology won't be of much value to your business.

Part I

Understanding the life cycle of a customer

"Give me six hours to chop down a tree, and I will spend the first four sharpening the axe."

-Abraham Lincoln

One of the biggest concerns of business owners today is maintaining customer loyalty. Without customers, your business has nothing, regardless of how good your product or service may be.

Developing that loyalty has become ever more difficult.

The democratization of information has created an increasingly competitive landscape for most businesses today. With virtually limitless information at the fingertips of your customers and prospects, it is a challenge to keep your product or service from becoming completely commoditized.

The sobering reality is that the typical business will lose half of its customer base every five years. If you have a hundred customers today, and add no more, you will have fifty in five years. To put it another way, the first fifty customers you add over the next five years will merely serve to keep you where you are today.

If that doesn't startle you, think about how much you spend to bring in those new customers. The cost of acquiring a new customer can be seven to ten times more than the cost of retaining an existing one.

You can quickly see how a small increase in customer loyalty and retention can make a big difference on your bottom line. To succeed in this endeavor, you will need to evaluate and fine-tune your core business processes.

The key elements of any business process are your prospects and customers – without them you wouldn't have a business. Centering your objectives on acquiring new customers and retaining more of those you already have will help your business to grow and thrive in a competitive market.

Think of your customers as having a lifecycle with the following stages:

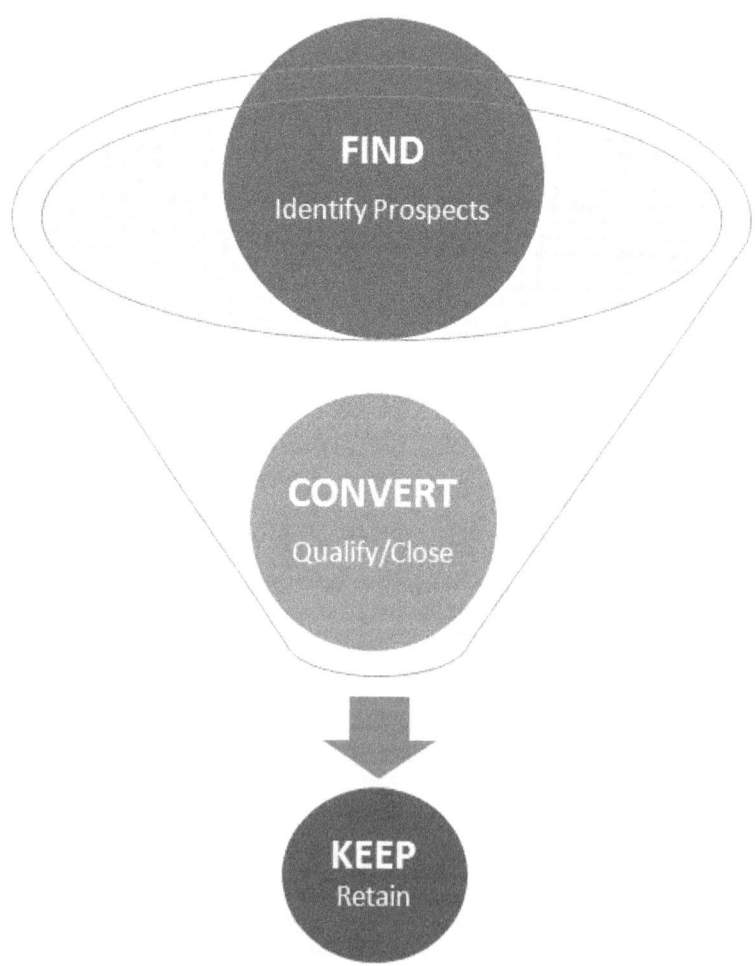

A complete set of business processes will include defined work flows that will address each of those three phases of the customer lifecycle.

At the beginning of the customer lifecycle, there are various methods you may be using to find qualified prospects. Identifying them is an essential first step, whether you purchase a list of prospects, get their names at a trade show, use social media to attract leads (blogs, twitter, Facebook, LinkedIn, etc.), or capture them directly from your website using a Web form.

The buzzword for this today is "lead generation." Times have changed, and it has become much less productive to take the same approaches for lead generation that have worked in the past. The numbers show that response rates aren't what they used to be, whether you use an unfocused direct mail campaign, generic email blasts, or a good old-fashioned telemarketing campaign. It is easy to spend a lot of time and money on things that worked in the past but don't work today.

A full discussion on lead generation is beyond the scope of this book, but it is important to consider a few of the basics as we look at the customer lifecycle.

Before you jump into a full-fledged lead generation program, it helps to create a plan. Here are some essential questions to help you define the best approach for your business:

What is the profile of your ideal customer?

How would you identify your target market(s)?

What are the needs of this target market?

What is the content of your marketing message?

What media do you plan to use in your multi-pronged marketing plan?

What activity and revenue goals will you use to measure your success?

What system/database do or will you use to track and manage the leads that you generate?

What lead nurturing plan do you have in place to handle leads who are not ready to buy today?

A successful lead generation program is an essential element of any company and will ensure your long-term success. In their book *Conquer the Chaos*, Clate Mask and Scott Martineau summarize this well:

"Growing is the only way to retain any control over your business. You have to fight. You have to get more customers. There is no maintaining: there is only growing. Without growth the world will pass you by."

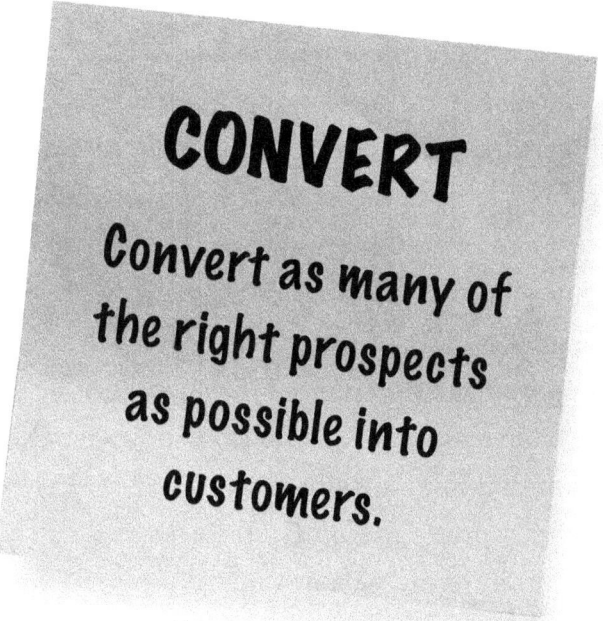

CONVERT

Convert as many of the right prospects as possible into customers.

"Don't spend so much time trying to choose the perfect opportunity," Michael Dell said, "that you miss the right opportunity." The goal of any business is to convert as many of the right prospects as possible into paying customers. The more organized and efficient you are in this phase, the more prospects you can effectively move through your sales process so they become customers.

You must be both efficient and persistent in the sales process. Every time I look at a broad set of sales statistics, I am reminded that winning in this stage of the customer lifecycle is not possible without a heavy dose of persistence. You could have the best product and a great value proposition and message, but unless you generate enough "touches" with your prospects, you won't reach the conversion rates you need to succeed. These touches include actually asking for the order.

It's estimated that only 19 percent of sales close in the first four contacts or touches. The remaining 81 percent close on or after the fifth one. Many businesses I speak to know this, yet few have a plan in place to ensure they are "showing up to the party" often enough to give themselves a chance to break out of the 19 percent bracket.

According to Dartnell Corp., 90 percent of businesses follow up with their prospects four times or fewer, and only 10 percent follow up five times or more. It doesn't take a math wizard to figure out who is getting most of the business. Don't waste all that time and effort on the front end and stop short of the finish line. Be sure to get in those five or more touches and contacts with your prospects.

The only way to ensure success in this area is to have a centralized database that can automate some of these required touches, track the notes and history of interactions with the prospect, and assign tasks at the appropriate time to ensure the sales rep can be visible at the right times to help move the sales process forward to closure.

The more prospects a sales rep must juggle to reach goals, the more precious this commodity of time becomes. A good sales rep learns how to quickly begin qualifying a prospect, while at the same time building rapport. And through the process, a good sales rep also knows several great trial closes they can use to ask for the order.

A good CRM system will help to organize, track, and execute all of this for you.

You've created an effective and efficient sales process and are converting a good ratio of prospects into customers. The next challenge is to develop a consistent and repeatable process that will best serve them and ensure you never let a customer relationship slip through the cracks.

Successful customer retention is interwoven into the entire customer lifecycle. It starts with the first contact you have with a prospect and continues the lifetime of the relationship. Customer retention is more than giving the customers what they expect; it's about exceeding their expectations so that they become loyal advocates for your product or service.

Harry Beckwith, author of *What Clients Love*, has a great philosophy that he calls "Your Three Key Moments: 3, 24, 5." Explaining the numbers, he makes the following points:

Research shows that the first **three seconds** of interaction with a client influences the level of their satisfaction more than the amount of service time that follows for that interaction.

When clients received a follow-up within **24 hours** of any interaction or request, a study found, they enjoyed a 40 percent higher level of satisfaction.

Sending a handwritten note within **five days** after a significant interaction is another great way to increase customer satisfaction.

Businesses come in all shapes and sizes, serve different markets, offer all sorts of products and services – but to run efficiently and grow over the long run, you need to focus on effectively managing the three phases of the customer lifecycle.

For success, a business must develop specific systems that ensure consistent performance in each phase. We will look closer at what this can mean to you in your business. We will help you identify what you're already doing well, what needs improvement, and what's missing in your various processes.

After you have reviewed what your business currently does well and what needs to be improved in each phase, you will begin to see the customer lifecycle in a more detailed and accurate way. You will see, with a much clearer focus, where you are and what you need to do to succeed and grow your business.

The old rules of marketing have given way to a new set of rules dictated by the proliferation of the Web. More people than ever are searching the Web to help them make all sorts of buying decisions. Various studies have found that a large percentage of business owners use the Web as an essential part of their research as they prepare to make a purchase.

This trend has been in place long enough that it is hardly new. In a 2004 article in *Forbes* (*"A Day in the Life of C-Level Executives, Part V," Forbes, September 2004*), companies were asked what they considered to be the most important source of business information. They found that:

- 49 percent of C-level executives said the Internet.
- 57 percent of large corporation senior management said the Internet.
- 85 percent of all participants in the survey said they used search engines to find business information.

This reality should tell you that you want to focus a good portion of your lead generation efforts on the Web. This may be a new area of lead generation for many small businesses, and like anything new, it can seem a bit overwhelming.

The good news is that with anything in business, it is possible to develop and follow a system and processes that will help you to deliver good results. Generating leads on the Web is no exception. A number of great books on this subject outline a foundation for a system proven to work.

Most websites are like online brochures and simply broadcast a message using the equivalent of a megaphone, Brian Halligan, the CEO and founder of Hubspot, says in his book *Inbound Marketing*.

Instead, he says, create a "marketing hub" that encourages interaction, a site where like-minded people can connect, moving away from the one-way sales message.

Halligan has a very practical approach to your website and believes that you should save the time and money on redesigning it entirely. He instead suggests a three-pronged approach to turning your site into a hub for prospects and customers alike.

1. Add something collaborative to your site, such as a blog.
2. Create lots of compelling content that people will want to consume.
3. Focus your efforts on where the real action is: Google, industry blogs, and social media sites.

If you can turn your website into a hub of compelling information, you will begin to attract more traffic. Now that you have the traffic, you will need to offer compelling reasons for visitors to "raise their hand" and ask for more information.

That can easily be done by offering industry articles, whitepapers, webinars, free trials, etc. A good website will have a handful of compelling calls to action where you offer further information that visitors will perceive as valuable in their search for information.

To get access to this compelling information, the visitor completes a short web form that should include (at a minimum) the visitor's name and email address. You have now added a lead to your system. It's time to begin a dialog as you work to nurture that lead into a good customer.

Before jumping right into a lead generation program, you must first identify exactly what the prospects and ultimately the customers will look like. Only by gaining that clear picture of whom you are looking for will you be able to develop and implement a successful lead generation program.

Below are some of the first steps in doing so. We will go into more detail in Chapter 7; for now, let's lay the foundation for creating and implementing your lead generation plan.

Create a profile of your ideal customer.
> Evaluate the traits of your best and worst customers, and rank them by profitability. Find common traits among the top five.

Identify your target market(s).
> From the profile you created, you now can evaluate where your target market exists. This will help you work so much smarter in your efforts to find and attract quality prospects.

Outline the needs of this target market.

This will help you to shape your messaging to ensure that you are conveying a value proposition that resonates with your target audience. This is essential for maximizing the conversion of qualified prospects.

Develop the content of your message.

Include core information that will effectively deliver your value proposition (articles, blog posts, e-books, whitepapers, etc.). You will use such information across multiple media as you work your lead generation plan.

Outline your multi-pronged marketing plan.

How will you work to get your message out to your target audience? A multi-pronged marketing approach works best in any lead generation program. In today's saturated and competitive markets, you can't survive on a single marketing medium. The more approaches you take, the more consistent you will be at generating new leads.

Set goals so you can measure your success.

How many leads are you trying to generate for a given period (week, month, quarter, year)? What new revenue goals are to trying to achieve from your lead generation program over a given period?

How to become visible on the Web

Now that we have identified the ingredients for your lead generation plan, let's get back to what is arguably the single most important medium in your lead generation platform – your website.

I believe that your website will continue to grow in its importance for generating those all important leads, so carefully consider the following facts, statistics and tips. This information is enough to get you started, but do yourself and your business a favor and commit to learning a lot more in this area.

If you invest the time to learn and hopefully even master this area of marketing, you can and will pass your competition by as your business becomes more and more visible on the web.

Google is by far the most widely used search engine on the market today, with over 65 percent of the world's search volume. If there is one place you want to focus to gain better visibility on the Web, it is Google.

There are basically two ways you can get your company to come up in the search results whenever someone seeks information related to what your business does or offers. Your company can appear in the "organic" search results (which are free), or you can purchase ads through Google's Adwords service in order to appear in the results.

Each of these two distinctly different types of search rankings comes with its own label and unique set of formulas for success.

- **SEM**, or "Search Engine Marketing," encompasses the "paid" method of ranking for certain keywords that a user might type. Next time you search for something on Google, pay attention to the layout of the page. Typically the top few search results are paid ads through Google Adwords. You will also see paid ads down the right-hand side of the screen. Google Adwords is an advertising service where you "pay-per-click" (PPC). Every time someone clicks on your ad to read more about what you have to offer, you will pay a fee for that click.

The general concept of Google Adwords is really quite simple:

- You create your ad and then tell Google what keywords you would like to trigger your ad.
- After you have the ad written and have identified the keywords, you are now ready to tell Google the maximum amount you are willing to bid each time someone clicks on your ad. (Remember, this is a pay-per-click service.)
- The amount you are willing to bid for each click, the relevance of your ad to that keyword, and the level

of competition will ultimately determine where your ad will appear in the list of ads competing for that given keyword.

Google Adwords can be a great way to get immediate visibility on the Web. Depending on the industry you are in and the level of competition, it can be expensive to get any meaningful ranking and visibility. The expression "you have to pay to play" really applies here.

It is estimated that 89 percent of all organic searches click through on the top 10 listings – which essentially represents the first page of search results. If you are not on the first page of search results, then only about 11 percent of the total traffic searching for what you have to offer may even notice your listing.

With this sobering reality and depending on your budget to be able to "play" in your space, it is a smart idea to learn how to capitalize on Google's free ranking method – SEO.

- **SEO**, or "Search Engine Optimization," is the free method of gaining visibility on the Web. If you create compelling content, Google will view your company and website as relevant and important for anyone searching for such content. The more relevant your content becomes in the Google world, the higher you will rank when someone searches for your related keywords and key phrases. Not only can you gain this ranking for free, but you pay nothing for all the clicks to your site. This is the single largest benefit of generating compelling content for your target audience.

Bottom line: Prove you have something meaningful to offer those searching for information in your space, and Google will help you get in front of all those people – free of charge.

A final compelling point: Organic search rankings (SEO) are more effective at getting clicks than paid ads (SEM). Research from Marketing Sherpa and Enquiro show that 75 percent of searchers click on SEO organic listings, while 25 percent click on the SEM paid results. These findings were detailed in the following Web pages:

http://www.hubspot.com/organic-vs-paid-search/

http://www.enquiroresearch.com/eyetracking-report.aspx

Hubspot offers a great free tool called Website Grader that will give you a thorough report on the current SEO strength of your website. This report will answer questions like: How well is your website doing? Is it getting traffic? Does it have SEO problems? How popular is it in social media?

I highly recommend that you start with Website Grader (http://websitegrader.com/) to get a detailed assessment of your website along with several ideas for improving your overall visibility on the Web.

There are several good books on this. Here are a few that I have read:

- *Inbound Marketing* by Brian Halligan
- *Get to the Top on Google* by David Viney

What's remarkable about the "find" phase of the customer lifecycle is the synergy: Your efforts feed on one another to increase your presence on the Web. As you build up steam, you gain momentum and generate more quality leads for your business.

We just talked about the value of improving your organic search ranking. The more great content you generate, the more attention you will garner from other sites linking to you and your content. Google will take notice and begin indexing your additional pages of great content, and at the end of the day you will gain more relevance and credibility in your space – which will result in higher search rankings.

Joe Pulizzi, in his book, *Get Content. Get Customers*, (coauthored by Newt Barrett), says it this way:

"The one who has the most engaging content wins, because frequent and regular contact build a relationship." And once you have that relationship with prospects, you have plenty of opportunities to convert them to customers.

"Advertising is a luxury," he writes, "but content is survival."

Good content creates a competitive advantage

Ann Handley and C.C. Chapman, in their book *Content Rules*, quote an owner of a swimming pool installation company:

"Today, I see my business as a content marketing company. In other words, my entire goal is to give more valuable, helpful, and remarkable content to consumers than anyone else in my field, which will in turn lead to more sales."

If you can deliver the answers to your prospect's questions, and keep them engaged with good content throughout their buying process, and if you do this better than your competition, you are in a much better position to win their business.

Several good books tell how to create such winning content. Here are a few that I have read:

- *Web Copy That Sells* by Maria Veloso
- *Content Rules* by Ann Handley & C.C. Chapman

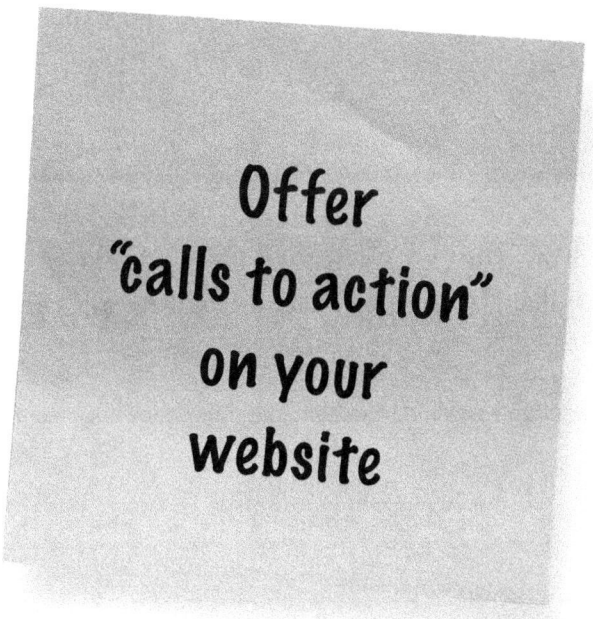

As you create your content, always keep in mind that your goal is to drive some sort of action. You can create good content that also delivers a compelling call to action. The goal is to generate a "conversion" that results when the visitor takes a desired action on your website. For example, the visitor might download an article or whitepaper, start a free trial, or request a demo.

Take some time to outline how ready your visitors are to become customers. Think of this in stages. You have "early-stage" visitors who are simply gathering general information, "mid-stage" visitors who are getting closer to a purchase and narrowing down a list of vendors to consider. Finally, the "late-stage" visitor is focusing on three or four vendors and is ready for demos on the finer points of each offering.

Your site needs to contain calls to action that cater to each of the stages you identify. After you have identified these buying stages and crafted the right calls to action to maximize "conversion" at each stage, you must then determine where on your site to place these calls to action.

Bottom line: The better you align the right calls to action at the right places on your website, the higher your conversion rates will be.

Here are a few good books on creating compelling calls to action that I have read:

- *Call to Action: Secret Formulas to Improve Online Results* by Bryan and Jeffrey Eisenberg
- *Landing Page Optimization: The Definitive Guide to Testing and Tuning for Conversions* by Tim Ash

Every lead generation program, no matter how targeted it might be, will generate a number of good leads who are simply not ready to do anything at the moment – yet it's still worth your effort to stay in touch with them.

You cannot easily or effectively nurture leads over time without incorporating some sort of automated system. There are many options on the market today, with a vast range of prices and capabilities.

Depending on your staff and budget, you may want to start with a basic e-mail marketing program. With such a program, you can load lists of leads and queue up ongoing campaigns to continue a conversation with these leads so you're top of mind when they are ready to buy. The cost of these basic email marketing programs varies a bit, but at the end of the day you can figure that you will be looking at an average cost of 1 to 2 cents per email sent.

The other end of the spectrum includes Marketing Automation Platforms, which can get complicated and expensive, especially for a small business. For a monthly fee ranging from $500 to $5,000, you can implement an automated system that will deliver an arsenal of tools for your lead nurturing efforts including:

- Email Marketing
- Campaign Reporting
- Landing Pages
- Lead Scoring
- Sales Alerts
- CRM Integration

There's good news though! A full-featured CRM system will have built-in email marketing tools that allow you to set up and manage aspects of your email marketing campaigns.

At BigContacts, we offer an "Autopilot" module for some of your email marketing. Let's say a lead visits your website and fills out a Web form to request information or start a free trial.

BigContacts can automate several aspects of that transaction.

- Load the contact information into your system
- Assign the contact to a member of your team
- Assign a task for that team member to follow up with the new lead
- Create a sales opportunity at the appropriate stage in your sales process
- Automatically queue up and begin sending a series of customized email messages over a given period.

You set all this up on the front end, and our system automatically and seamlessly executes your directions. Things happen exactly as you want at the right time – every time.

Bottom line: A successful lead generation program is an essential element of any company and will ensure your long-term success.

Identify a system to manage your leads

After you have invested the time and money to get your lead generation plan in place, don't make the mistake we see so many companies make. Make sure you have a foolproof system for capturing and organizing all your leads.

It is easy for leads to fall into a black hole, never to be seen again, if there is no real system in place to capture, organize and track every lead to ensure a timely follow-up.

I believe the best system for handling all the necessary moving parts in this process is CRM Software. Don't try doing it with an Excel spreadsheet. That approach can work to a point, but it is almost guaranteed that you will outgrow the spreadsheet and need to upgrade if you hope to continue growing. Avoid this inevitable growing pain and make the investment today in a good CRM system that will meet your specific business needs now and into the future.

Furthermore, don't limit flexibility and ultimate mobility for your company and your sales team. Invest in a Web-based system that will give you access to real-time information from anywhere you have an Internet connection.

It's estimated that the average cost of an onsite sales call is nearly $400, and these costs continue to rise. A good CRM System can help to increase the productivity of your sales team, containing or even decreasing your overall cost of sales.

That can be achieved through the effective collection, organization and dissemination of important contact information. Couple this organization with the automation of certain marketing functions, and your sales team can spend more time in front of prospects and clients doing what they do best – selling. With the information they have at their fingertips, they can also improve the quality of their sales calls.

What does your sales process look like? Have you taken the time to write it out, test it, and refine it over time?

A detailed discussion on selling techniques is outside of the scope of this book, but it is important to outline the four general stages of the selling process (questioning, presenting, overcoming objections, and closing the sale) along with some best practices for each stage. You need enough information to be effective at managing the "convert" stage of the customer lifecycle.

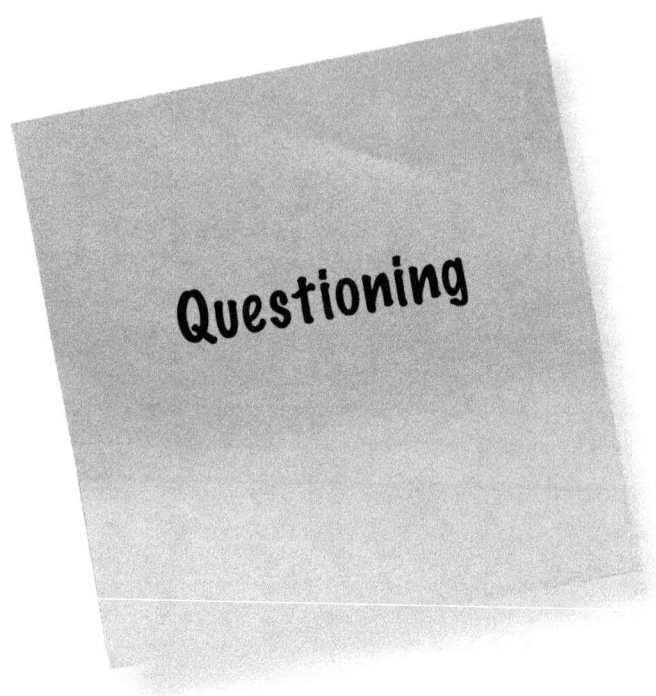

A set of well-planned questions is the foundation on which you build any sales process. Questioning is your first and best opportunity to get inside the mind of your prospects to understand how they think, learn what's important to them, identify where their pain points are, and learn how much they will actually be influencing the sale.

Below is a good template for questioning that can work for virtually any sales process. This template offers a logical and effective order of questions to help move the sales process along efficiently.

Key questions for your sales process

Current situation. Find out what the prospect is doing today as it relates to the product or service you offer.

Current needs. Determine the prospect's pain points and rank them in order of priority.

Decision-making process. Find out who needs to be involved to make the decision, what criteria they will use, and when they plan to make the decision.

Competition. Even though the prospect may have already mentioned a competitor during your conversations, don't skip this important step. Find out about all competitors so you know how best to position your solution so that the prospect views it favorably compared to the others.

Budget. Depending on the expense of your solution and how it compares to your competition, you want to know what the prospect can invest in your product or service. Make sure the prospect is at least in your ballpark before you go further, or you may end up wasting a lot of your time.

Now that you have the key questions that you can ask to effectively qualify your prospects, make sure to listen. The key to success here is to make sure that you are not just hearing what you want to hear but in fact are really hearing what the prospect is saying. It's through this active and genuine listening that you can differentiate yourself from the competition, which may not be listening to the prospect.

To make sure you are hearing what you think you are and to let the prospect know you really are listening, paraphrase what the prospect is telling you in the form of a question at appropriate times during your conversation.

A simple yet effective example of how to do this would be:

"Let me make sure I understand you correctly. You _____"
(Restate what you just thought you heard, to gain affirmation from the prospect.)

Take all the great insights you have just gathered about your prospect and load them into the contact record in your CRM system. The more prospects you deal with, the more important this becomes.

You want to be able to clear your mind to work freely with each and every prospect that you come in contact with, but you don't want to forget anything that will help you win a deal. Getting this important detail loaded into your CRM system will ensure that this information is always at your fingertips and ready for your review when it comes time to prepare and present your solution.

Armed with the right insights and a true picture of the prospects' needs, you are in a position of strength to create and deliver a presentation that truly speaks to their needs.

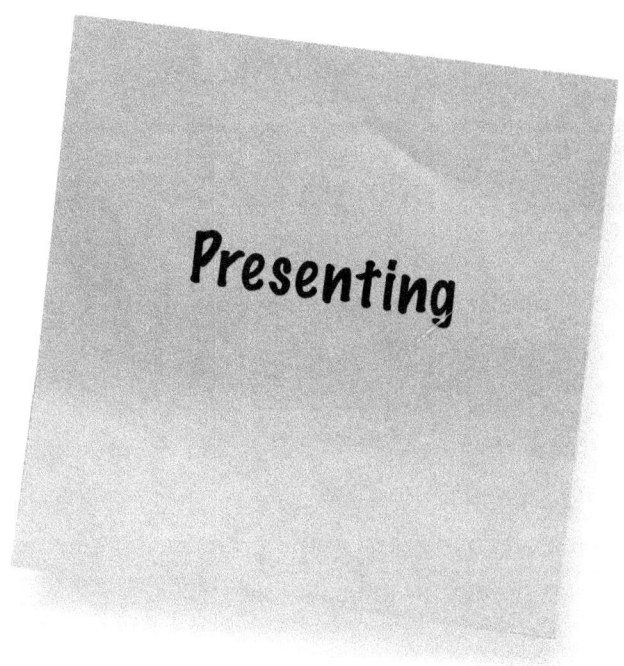

You have successfully navigated the first few stages of the sales process. You now have some rapport and trust built with your prospect, and those with the power to make a decision have agreed to a presentation to see exactly what you can do for them. This is one of the most important points in the whole process, and it's up to you to make a compelling pitch.

You have them right where you want them. They are open and receptive to allowing you to educate them on the value that your company can deliver to meet their needs. If you're prepared, you now have an opportunity to shine and show your prospects that you have listened and understand their needs and then illustrate your company's competitive advantage.

Unfortunately, this is a pivotal opportunity in the sales process that too many salespeople leave to chance. It's show time! This is your chance to finally win them over and shut out the competition. You must prepare for this meeting.

Preparing your sales presentation

Determine the type of presentation that will be most appropriate for this deal.

Research the people who will attend the presentation.

Review all your notes on this prospect and determine what to focus on in your presentation.

Organize all the content for your presentation and create your slides, etc.

Rehearse the presentation to ensure it flows in a way to deliver the most impact.

Once you have it just where you want it... **practice, practice, practice.**

This last part is never fun, and as a result, most salespeople aren't willing to do what it takes to really nail the presentation. That's actually good – provided you are one of the few who *will* put in the time. You will win more deals by practicing to ensure that you have nailed the essence and flow of the presentation, as this will win over more prospects than you can imagine.

A well-rehearsed presentation with the right information high-lighted will allow you to effectively present all the key points you need to make it obvious what your competitive advantages are. The experience of a well-delivered presentation can actually take a slightly inferior product or service and elevate it enough to help you win over a better product or service that was not presented as skillfully as yours.

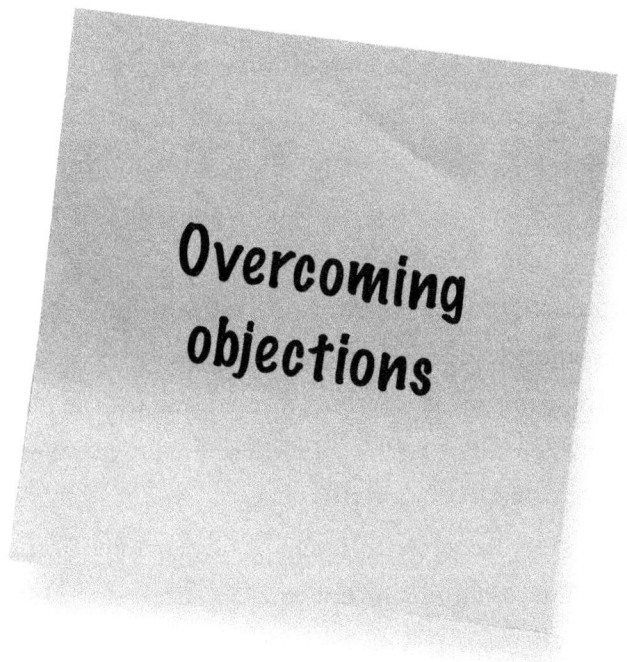

During the sales process you have identified needs, and it's quite likely that you have already handled a number of questions or objections as they came up. It's toward the end of the sales process when things are logically coming to a head that the hidden objections can begin to surface.

You may feel as if you have already handled all the objections when a zinger is launched at you in this late stage. That's OK. Remain calm and keep in mind that an objection is still an opportunity to close.

Josiane Chriqui Feigon, author of a great sales book called *Smart Selling on the Phone and Online*, has an excellent chapter on handling objections. In Chapter 8 of her book, she helps you gain a better understanding of where objections can come from, what you might be doing to cause some of them, and what you can do to greatly reduce them throughout the sales process.

Notice that I used the word "reduce" here and not "eliminate." It's almost impossible to eliminate all objections. Feigon leaves you with a gift that she calls the "Comeback Pack." She lists the most common objections that you have likely heard if you have been selling for any length of time. In this list she then arms you with several "comebacks" that you can use.

"The rebuttal questions," she says, "are not just defensive statements: they are specifically designed to help you better understand exactly where the prospect stands so that you can use the objection as an opportunity to create rapport and keep moving through the sales cycle."

What a great resource to have as a salesperson. You can pick from a long list of options to find the questions that best fit your selling style. Whatever you do, pick them, memorize them, and use them every time that particular objection comes up, and you will find much greater success in defusing common objections.

The best scenario you could ask for when closing the sale is that the prospect makes his or her own decision to buy because it simply seems like the logical thing to do based upon all of the information you and your company have provided.

Your success in closing the sale isn't about some last-minute decision where the customer decides to go with your product or service. The ultimate decision the prospect makes to buy from you is based on how well your selling process matched his buying process.

The backbone of a good selling process includes these key ingredients:

Summary of a successful sales process

Ask good questions

Listen carefully to the answers

Present information in a way that resonates

Handle objections with solid answers

Close the sale as a result of this effective process

This is where you won the business. It was a result of a well-orchestrated sales process that met the prospect's needs during the buying process.

To compete in today's markets, most all businesses have faced the challenge of moving from a product-oriented to a customer-oriented model. CRM software can be a very effective tool in making that change.

If implemented correctly, CRM maximizes the lifetime value of the customers you have today and those you will bring on board tomorrow. To succeed, businesses must understand that they will need to design, implement and manage a solution. They must align their people, processes and technology to the new customer-centric model.

An important ingredient for maximizing the lifetime value of each client is in the processes you execute at every customer touch point. CRM software can then consolidate and organize all this information that your company gathers on customers and prospects. Properly organizing it will give you the insights you need to effectively handle these relationships.

CRM software can help you improve your customer service and reduce customer churn in different ways, depending on your company, customers, the product you sell, and the way you sell it. But to effectively leverage CRM in your business you will need the flexibility to tailor the software to more closely align with your overall company strategy.

A company can differentiate itself with a very good product or service, but that rarely lasts forever. Even a great product will eventually run into enough competition to easily become more of a commodity. The best way to defend any position is to employ a good offense. The best offense is to consistently deliver excellent customer service along with a great product.

It's been documented that many customers find more value in the level of support they receive than in the finer details of the actual product or service. A CRM platform that is well-matched to your particular business needs is a fundamental part of a successful customer service strategy.

Have you evaluated your customer retention rate? Do you have a plan to keep more of your customers? Have you implemented any technology solutions to help you in your customer retention efforts?

Below are some statistics that will motivate any business owner to take steps to develop and implement a solid customer service initiative.

- Only one out of 25 dissatisfied customers will express dissatisfaction, so don't lull yourself into complacency by thinking your business is immune. You have to take action in this area to protect and grow your customer base.

- Happy customers tell four or five others of their positive experience. Dissatisfied customers tell nine to twelve how bad it was. Bad news travels farther and wider than good news. It's human nature.

- The average company loses 10 percent of its customers each year. At that rate you will turn over half of your existing customer base in five years. Whatever you can do to reduce that percentage will greatly impact your bottom line.

- Acquiring new customers can cost five times more than satisfying and retaining current customers, so do every thing you can to embrace your current customers. Your long-term growth and profitability depend on it.

- The longer you retain customers, the more the profitability tends to increase.

Here is further confirmation of the importance of implementing a successful customer retention strategy. According to the U.S. Small Business Administration and the U.S. Chamber of Commerce, customers leave for the following reasons:

Why do Customers Leave?
68% leave because they are unhappy with the level of customer service.
14% are dissatisfied with the product or service.
9% choose to start doing business with a competitor.
3% move to another area of the country.
1% die.

If you keep in mind that there is more to business than a transaction, and if you work to build a relationship with your customers, you can strengthen your bond with them. As we have seen, the long-term success of your business depends in large part on the percentage of your current customers who choose to stay with you.

The next time they decide to spend money on the kind of services you offer, you want to be their first choice. Your customers may even be willing to pay more for your product or service if they have a personal connection with your company.

The ingredients for building strong relationships with your customers are not a big secret. Most of the principles for success in life are pretty straightforward. The costs of implementing a successful retention program are relatively low, as it mainly involves your time.

The challenge lies in the execution of your plan. Successful execution requires a combination of people and technology. We will take a closer look at how best to execute your plan a bit later. Let's first take a look at some of the essentials for increasing customer retention.

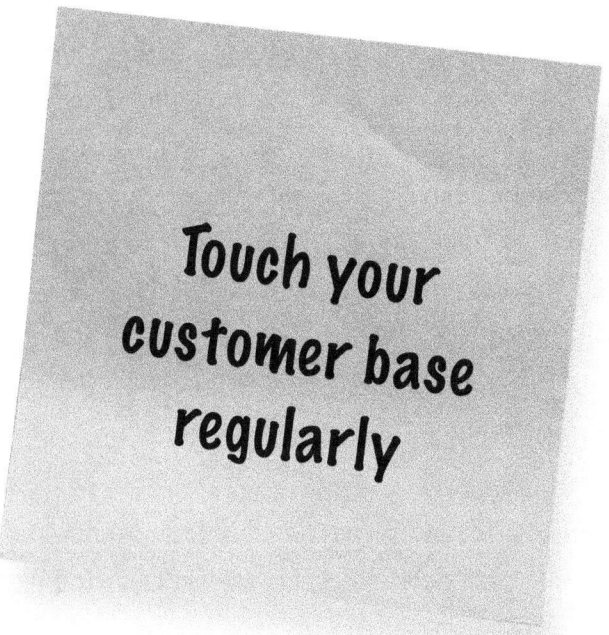

There are many opportunities during the lifecycle of your customers to reach out and show them that you value their business and that you are thinking of them.

- **New business** – Just after your customers place an order or you have provided them with a service, ask for their feedback. Letting them know that you care about their level of satisfaction says a lot about your commitment to their relationship as a customer. It can also provide you with an opportunity to gain insight on other products and services that you could offer to gain new business.

- **Ongoing education** – How complex and involved is your product or service? It's important to consider the need to re-educate your customers over time. It may be one of the most influential things you can do to ensure that what you offer is adopted and used long term.

- **Product updates** – Whether a customer has already purchased a certain product from you or has never heard of it, it's a good idea to keep him or her up-to-date on what you are doing and what you have to offer. This will ensure that you will be top-of-mind the next time the customer is ready to make a purchase of this sort.

- **Special offers** – Everyone loves a deal! From time-to-time a well-timed special offer may be just what you need to motivate your customers to make another purchase.

- **Check in** – If a customer has not done business with you in a while, check to see how you can help. It may also serve as a reminder that the customer needs your product or service.

All of this might seem a bit overwhelming. You may be saying to yourself, "I am already maxed out, overworked and overloaded. How on earth can I possibly implement all of this follow-up without hiring more people that I can't afford to hire?"

That's a valid concern, but you can automate much of this through a good CRM and email marketing program. The combination of these platforms will allow you to place much of the ongoing touch points with your customers on autopilot.

If set up correctly, all of this can run in the background automatically to deliver the following benefits to your company:

- You will be able to effectively handle and stay on top of more customers.

- You can create the impression that you personally sent the email, or newsletter, to each and every one of your customers.

- You can rest assured that nothing will fall through the cracks again as you are now able to deliver a consistent, timely and personalized message to your customers when and how needed.

While it is true that you can manage a lot of your customer communication using email, it's still important to pick up the phone occasionally and actually call your customers. Nothing can fully replace personal communication when it comes to building long-term relationships. I have great news for you here, too: A good CRM system will automate the tasks to remind you when to actually pick up the phone and make those important calls.

The best way to prove your commitment to delivering a high level of service is through your actions. When a customer has an issue or needs technical assistance, make it your priority to resolve it immediately. Every time an issue is resolved in a timely manner, you will build the confidence your customers have in your company to deliver what they need. Prompt follow-up is a great opportunity to show your commitment to the customer, and turn a potentially bad situation into a real positive one.

Let's say you have made all the right changes and have now turned your customer service/support center into an asset for your company. You're now in a position to turn this into an area that can actually generate more revenue for your company.

With the right approach and the right information at their fingertips (by using a good CRM system), your customer service and support team now has the opportunity to cross sell or up-sell the existing customers that they support. If done right, this part of your business can transform from a pure overhead item to a profit center.

An essential part of any client retention program involves direct feedback from your customers.

There are a variety of ways to gather feedback from your customers, but one of the most efficient and effective tools we have used is a customer survey. It wasn't too long ago that the common practice was to send a survey in the mail. You sent it out and then waited for your customers to mail it back to you.

Today, there are a number of great, easy-to-use survey tools that allow you to simply email the survey, collect the data electronically and gain a good picture of where things are. All without licking a stamp or running off to the post office with a box full of envelopes.

This function should be a built-in tool in the suite of tools that you use to manage the customers' lifecycle.

A well-written survey can provide invaluable insights into what your customers like and dislike about your product or service. This information can help shape anything from the direction you take in your product development to the way you deliver customer service. Listening closely to this feedback and acting upon it will go a long ways to increasing your customer retention over the long run. If your customers share their complaints with you in this process, that's a very good thing.

What can you gather from a survey?

Customer satisfaction: Find out what your customers think about your product or service.

Company insight: Identify any improvements that you could make to increase satisfaction for both your customers AND employees – as your employees ultimately influence customer satisfaction.

Evaluate the competition: Find out what other companies your customers may like and what they like about them.

According to 1st Financial Training Services, 96 percent of customers don't complain, they just leave. Of those that leave, 91 percent will never come back.

Finally, surveys are also effective with former customers. If you can find patterns for why they left in the first place, you can work to improve the experience for current customers.

No matter how well your product or service ranks in your specific marketplace, you can grow your business by mastering the customer lifecycle.

If you put the right processes and technology in place you can outmaneuver, outsmart and outshine your competition – all without improving one thing about your product.

Getting this critically important aspect of your business right will ensure that you have a healthy business for many years to come.

Part II

Managing the customer life cycle with CRM software

"Information is a source of learning. But unless it is organized, processed, and available to the right people and in the right format for decision making, it is a burden and not a benefit."

–William Pollard

The ripple effect from today's tough economic times has forced virtually every business to reevaluate how it operates. When top-line revenues decline, it's important to evaluate your expenses to cut back where you can. The challenge is to do so while maintaining the level of service your customers have come to expect.

To navigate these tough waters, it's important to correctly distinguish between an expense and an investment when making decisions that affect the growth of your business. The numbers show that CRM software fits squarely in the investment category.

The bottom line is businesses that take care of their customers and consistently find new ones will be successful. The people most responsible for finding new customers and maintaining satisfied, profitable relationships with existing ones are salespeople.

Many CRM platforms try to be everything to everyone, offering accounting, project management, ticketing systems, and more. The most successful CRM software solutions are those specifically designed to help manage the sales process. And no matter what measure we look at, when that key focus is established and maintained, the positive results to both the top and bottom lines cannot be denied.

In any business or industry it's easy to forget that our customers may not know all the acronyms we develop and use so freely, so let's take a moment to define just what "CRM" means and the general options available to you today.

CRM (Customer Relationship Management) Software" is foundational software that will help organize and streamline any business. The "C" in CRM is what this software is all about – the "customer."

At its core, a good CRM system helps you attract and retain customers. It helps you to better understand their requirements and satisfy their needs. A well-designed system can help you to convert more prospects into customers, keep more of those you already have, and free up precious time to give you a better balance between work, family, and friends.

Does that sound dramatic? If you are skeptical that software can really do all this, read on: It has done so for my business and for several thousand that we have helped.

Before we examine the types of programs on the market today, let's take a quick look at how we got to where we are today.

According to the technical training website Exforsys.com, businesses did very little (before CRM software came along) to retain customers after the purchase. There wasn't any real sense of urgency to cater to the customers as it was widely thought, at least by larger companies, that they could easily replace their customers.

According to Merchantos.com, businesses began using databases in the 1980s to keep track of their clients and prospects, collecting and organizing information about them. This shift was driven by the fact that we were now entering the information age and everything about the consumer was changing. Consumers were becoming more aware of the products they were buying, and were now better equipped to evaluate alternative choices and the companies they were buying from.

Marketing was the primary goal, and the use of databases for that purpose was the beginning of what led to what we know as

CRM today. In the 1980s, some of the first iterations of CRM became available in the marketplace.

The term "Customer Relationship Management" actually wasn't developed until the 1990s. In that decade, the technology for CRM began to grow beyond basic "database marketing" and focus more on customer service and retention. The concept of CRM was quickly evolving.

The first few years of the 2000s saw CRM really come into its own. The programs were getting easier to use, more affordable and more customizable for businesses. It was becoming much easier to maintain and utilize important information about customers and prospects.

With a growing goal of managing the customer experience, CRM is here to stay, and its value to businesses will only increase. No matter how big or small, businesses must rely more and more on technology to help them collect, organize and analyze information about their customers. It's the foundation for converting and keeping more prospects.

Following is an overview of the general types of programs available for use in the small-business market today.

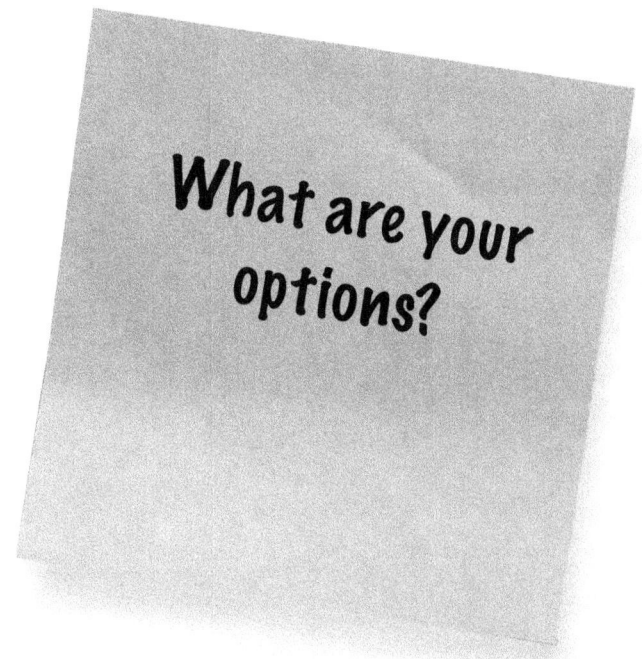

It's important to first understand the types of programs available. An appreciation of the strengths and weaknesses of each type will help you make the right decision for your business. While reviewing each type, we will look briefly at some of the important questions to ask as you begin your evaluations.

There are essentially two primary types of CRM programs that we see small businesses use in their quest to get more organized and to gain better control over their business:

- **PC-based CRM programs**
- **Web-based CRM programs**

PC-based CRM programs

We have all purchased "software in a box" at some point. You pull the CD out of the box and download the software on your computer, and in minutes you are enjoying your new purchase. That works just fine as long as you won't need to network this software through other computers or share any of the information with others in your company or team.

But if you do need to network and share the functionality of this software, you could quickly rack up significant up-front costs. The other cost, often overlooked, involves ongoing maintenance, support and software upgrades to ensure you have the latest and greatest. The total cost of ownership can easily run multiples of your initial purchase price.

Companies also may find that while traditional software can be customized, it often leads to version-lock and issues when trying to preserve changes through an upgrade. Simple upgrades can become costly, resource-intensive projects. To alleviate such headaches, software vendors may recommend that organizations limit or refrain from customizing the application and instead stick with the default, "off-the-shelf" settings.

Traditional software is challenged when it comes to meeting the needs of today's business. If you are considering a purchase of PC-based software, you will want to ask yourself these questions:

Will I have access to my contact data from the Web and my mobile phone?

A PC-based program does not allow you access from the Web or mobile phone. If you wish to network this software, it will likely require an additional investment in a consultant and some additional hardware.

Will the PC-based system allow my business to grow without additional investment?

Any time you wish to update your PC-based software to include new features, you are required to purchase the latest program. You also may need to spend money for a consultant if you have anything networked.

Is the software easy to use so my team can get off to a quick start? Does the company offer training, and what will it cost me?

Unless you're a one-person business, you will likely need to hire a consultant to help you set up and customize your system. Most PC-based software will include very limited support and will require you to invest additional sums to get any ongoing client support. I have seen programs charge $300 per year per user for their "enhanced client support" service.

How secure is my contact data?

It is likely that with any PC-based software, you will load the program on a laptop to give you mobility. Here are some startling statistics about your laptop:

- According to the FBI, a laptop is stolen every 53 seconds and 97 percent of those are never recovered.

- According to *Fast Company* magazine, more than 12,000 laptops disappear each week in U.S. airports alone. Only 3 percent of laptops are ever returned. http://www.fastcompany.com/magazine/130/to-catch-a-thief.html

- According to the Ponemon Institute, it costs a company a few hundred dollars per missing record when factoring in the loss of customers, legal fees, and PR crisis management. A few thousand records can quickly add up. http://www.ponemon.org/index.php

- "The loss of a laptop computer may well be quite expensive if it contains unencrypted confidential data," according to the 2008 CSI Computer Crime and Security Survey. In 2008, 42 percent of all corporate security incidents were because of a stolen laptop, second only to viruses and insider abuse. http://i.zdnet.com/blogs/csisurvey2008.pdf?tag=mantle_skin;content

If something crashes, how do I recover important information?

The security of your data is only as good as your own personal data recovery plan. Do you back up your data regularly? If so, where do you store it? Is your backup safe if your hard drive crashes?

Here are more facts to consider:

- According to American Data Recovery, hardware failure accounts for 78 percent of all data loss.

- According to FileSlinger, 1 in 5 computers will suffer a fatal hard drive crash during its lifetime.

- According to RackSpace, 50 percent of small businesses never fully recover from a data loss.

How does the company support the software? If support is not included in purchase price, how much is charged for it?

At BigContacts, we believe a set of support services needs to be in place as a minimum to ensure your success. That set of support tools and resources should be included in the cost of the software. If it's not, make sure the vendor clearly outlines what those services will cost on an ongoing basis.

Here are the minimum tools and resources I would recommend when you make your next CRM software investment:

- **Email ticketing system:** This will allow you to submit a request for issues that may be more involved or technical in nature or pertain to a possible bug. The ticketing system gives a ticket number and is tracked in the system to help ensure your support issue does not fall through the cracks.

- **Live chat:** This is a great service that allows you (during business hours) to ask a quick question and get instant feedback. It is great for those questions that are not as involved and require a quick answer to get you back on track with your CRM system.

- **Support library:** A good library of support resources should include:

> **Knowledge-base articles**, in which you can read practical "how to" reports on getting things done within your system.

> **Downloads** for user guides, best-practices papers.

> **Videos** to show you firsthand the best practices for using a variety of your CRM system's features.

This type of software requires no installation or up-front fees for purchase. Instead, you will find it sold on a subscription basis where you pay a monthly fee as a subscriber. Web based CRM software is sold and maintained as a service to the end-user. Software as a Service (SaaS) is a software distribution model in which applications are hosted by a vendor or service provider and made available to customers over a network, typically the Internet.

Most industry analysts agree that Software as a Service (SaaS) is not a fad and in fact is the next big step in the evolution of software.

- IDC predicts that the SaaS market as a whole will reach $40.5 billion by 2014, representing a compound annual growth rate of 25.3 percent. The market research firm goes on to predict that the top five SaaS applications that businesses are likely to pursue this year are collaboration applications, Web applications and Web serving software, cloud backup systems, business applications (ERP, CRM and human resource management), and personal productivity applications.

- About 30 percent of the businesses surveyed by the Computer Technology Industry Association plan to implement SaaS solutions this year to lower costs and "maintain their competitive edge." According to CompTIA, that is up from 22 percent and 14 percent respectively in the two prior years.

IDC captures this sentiment well in one of its recent SaaS studies: "The harsh economic climate will actually accelerate the growth prospects for the software-as-a-service (SaaS) model." The report says that this new delivery channel for software can be a great alternative to more traditional installed or "on-premise" software. Software delivered through the SaaS model can eliminate upfront costs, reduce ongoing maintenance costs and, in many cases, is much easier to use.

Software as a Service (SaaS) applications enjoy some very attractive benefits, and that's what will continue to drive the growth of this market.

Benefits of Software as a Service (SaaS)

Low or no up-front capital investment

Minimal IT investment and support needed

Ongoing, seamless updates and improvements

Rapid deployment

If you are considering a purchase of Web-based software, here are some questions to ask:

Will the Web-based software allow my business to grow without additional investment?

Carefully evaluate what you need today as well as what you might want soon. I have seen examples of what I think are just short of a "bait and switch" approach.

Often you can get started for a very reasonable price, but as your business and needs grow you may need to pay much more for access to important features your business requires.

Make sure you know what you get for your money, and understand the company's pricing model and philosophy for additional capacity and functionality you soon might need. The last thing you want to do is to get invested in a platform today with a certain budget in mind only to find that this budget increases exponentially as your needs change.

How easy is it to use? Is training available, and at what cost?

Some of the larger CRM applications on the market today can be a bit complicated and are not easy to adopt within your business. Because of the complexity, some of the larger providers in the market today employ small armies of consultants certified to help train you on their platform and to help you spend your money. The average rates in the market run about $75 per hour, so you and your team might want to learn fast.

On the other hand there are some good CRM applications that are very intuitive and easy to learn. Some offer free training to all your subscribers.

One of the key reasons that a new CRM initiative fails is lack of proper training across the organization. Find out exactly what training and support is included, and get it in writing if you can.

Is my contact data secure?

As you begin to evaluate the Web-based CRM providers, get the details about how they handle each of the following three elements of data security. You want to make sure the vendors you are considering are not skimping when it comes to the security and safety of your data. After all, what you're trying to protect here is only the most detailed and sensitive information about all of your customers!

Here are the three essential elements of security to consider when evaluating vendors:

1. Data encryption over the Internet (SSL)

If you have ever logged into your bank account online, you were almost certainly viewing that information through an encrypted (SSL) connection. At the Web address bar at the top of your screen, look at the address you are accessing. At the beginning of the address, you will see one of two formats: http:// or https://. The "https://" or SSL connection indicates it is encrypted, which you should require for sensitive customer data. SSL (Secure Socket Layer) is the Internet standard for establishing an encrypted connection between your browser and the Web server.

The primary reason SSL is used is to keep sensitive information sent across the Internet encrypted so only the intended recipient can understand it. This is important because the information you send on the Internet is passed from computer to computer to get to the destination server. Any computer in between you and the server can see your credit card numbers, user names and passwords, and other sensitive information if it is not encrypted with an SSL certificate. When an SSL certificate is used, the information becomes unreadable to everyone except for the server to which you are sending the information. This protects it from hackers and identity thieves.

PC   Internet   Web Server

In addition to encryption, a proper SSL certificate also provides authentication. This means you can be sure that you are sending information to the right servers with your CRM software provider. Why is this important? The nature of Web-based CRM software means you will be sending information through the Internet using your computer or mobile device. You want to ensure that the private information you are sending is secure.

2. Data center – A data center is the most important and vulnerable component of your Web-based CRM system. The data center is the physical location that houses the Web servers that will store and back up all your important prospect and customer data.

You want to know that any vendor you are considering is housing that important information in a secure and well-equipped data center.

3. Data backup – The safety of and reliable access to your data is the most important priority in our business. It is critical that you back up your entire database every night to ensure that you always have a very recent copy of your contact data.

My company, BigContacts, works only with the top companies in each of those three areas. Below are our key vendors who ensure the safety and security of your customer data. I like to think of this as a blueprint of what you should look for as you evaluate your next CRM software provider.

Data encryption

We work with Verisign, the most trusted and recognizable name in this aspect of the business.

VeriSign is the leading SSL certificate provider, enabling a secure connection between our Web servers and your Internet browser. Many feel that they are the most trusted mark on the Internet, with one of the strongest SSL encryptions available today.

VeriSign secures more than one million Web servers worldwide, more than any other certificate authority, and also serves the world's forty largest banks and over 95 percent of Fortune 500 companies with SSL certificates.

Data center

We're confident Rackspace will take care of us so that we can focus our time on taking care of our customers. Rackspace is the IT hosting leader. For nine years it has proven to be the leader in the hosting industry, setting the standard for what their customers can expect in customer service, technical support, expertise, network uptime and server availability. It's a standard that no other provider can promise, let alone deliver.

Gartner Inc. recognizes Rackspace as a leader in the hosting industry. Microsoft has designated it as the coveted Hosting Partner of the Year three times, more than any other provider.

With multiple redundancies built into its systems and numerous network providers delivering strictly high performance bandwidth to its data centers, Rackspace provides network performance and availability unequaled by other providers. That translates into maximum network uptime and reduced performance latencies for all of our customers. The data you need is available whenever you need it.

Rackspace provides maximum protection of your data by covering all three critical areas of security - physical, operational and system security. Rackspace's commitment to such comprehensive security gives us the confidence to know that we offer our customers the most secure solutions available.

Data backup

We work with two industry leaders to handle our data backup needs.

For all of your core contact history, we again rely on Rackspace to deliver unparalleled service.

In the aftermath of any disaster, whether manmade or natural, more than half of smaller businesses never recover from data loss. For large businesses, losing data that affects millions of customers and employees can be overcome. The recovery, however, will dramatically impact their revenue numbers and their brand reputations.

Every year, unrecoverable data loss costs businesses millions of dollars. More than ever it's vital to have a process, like managed data backups, in place to preserve your data, maintain its integrity, and keep your business operating unimpeded and without loss.

Rackspace's flexible and reliable Unmetered Managed Backup service delivers peace of mind by reducing your risk and restoring your data as quickly and completely as possible. It's all about ensuring the continuity of your business operations without your having to do much of anything, including worry.

In addition to the core contact history, BigContacts allows you to store important customer files and documents directly in a given contact record. We entrust the backup and safety of our file storage to Amazon's Web Services team.

Since early 2006, Amazon Web Services (AWS) has provided companies of all sizes with an infrastructure Web services platform in the cloud.

With AWS, they take advantage of Amazon.com's global computing infrastructure, which is the backbone of Amazon.com's $15 billion retail business and transactional enterprise. The scalable, reliable, and secure distributed computing infrastructure has been honed for over 13 years.

Amazon Web Services gives us a cost-effective solution for storing information in the cloud.

With Amazon S3, we get a highly reliable, data storage infrastructure that enables us to deliver cost-effective and dependable backup solutions for all our customers.

Your head may be spinning right now, and you might be asking if all this is really necessary. Only you can answer that question, so I like to turn it around and ask:

What would it cost your business if you lost all of your important prospect and customer data? What is your plan for recovery? And how long would it take you to get back to full speed again?

With a good Web-based CRM platform, you can do all of this for less than $1 per day for each user. Your data is worth many times that, so why settle for anything less?

Finally, when evaluating Web-based CRM software, you should ask about the available support, just as you would do in evaluating PC-based CRM systems:

What type of support is included in my purchase price? If it is not included, how much do you charge?

To ensure successful implementation and continued success, you need to know that you have sufficient support that you can count on.

Here again, we believe a minimum set of support services needs to be in place. They should be included in the cost of the software. Otherwise, the vendor should clearly outline the continuing cost.

Minimum support services should include an e-mail ticketing system, live chat, and a support library with knowledge-base articles, downloads and videos. They are the same support services detailed earlier for PC-based systems.

I have given a lot more time and ink to discussing Web-based CRM software than to PC-based products.

As the founder of a Web-based CRM software company, I firmly believe that this form of software is the most efficient and effective way for a small business to harness the power of technology that, until recently, was only available to larger enterprises.

The economy of scale that can be achieved through the Software as a Service model is so significant that you can now acquire very capable (enterprise-level) software for less than what you would have paid for basic PC-based software just a few years ago.

However, when choosing a Web-based CRM company, there is so much more that must be considered. There is a lot to know to ensure that you choose a vendor that has your best interests at heart and is willing to do what it takes to ensure that your data is as secure as possible.

Have you ever spent money on software for your business only to find out later that you did not realize the return on investment or improvement in efficiencies that you were told you could achieve and that you had counted on? The reason you were disappointed probably was because you didn't spend enough time identifying your specific needs.

As with any endeavor, it's difficult to achieve objectives if they are not clearly identified first. Take the time to get your thoughts on paper, and ultimately you and your business will benefit greatly.

A well-thought-out CRM business plan will help you to plan for and address some of the key roadblocks to a successful implementation.

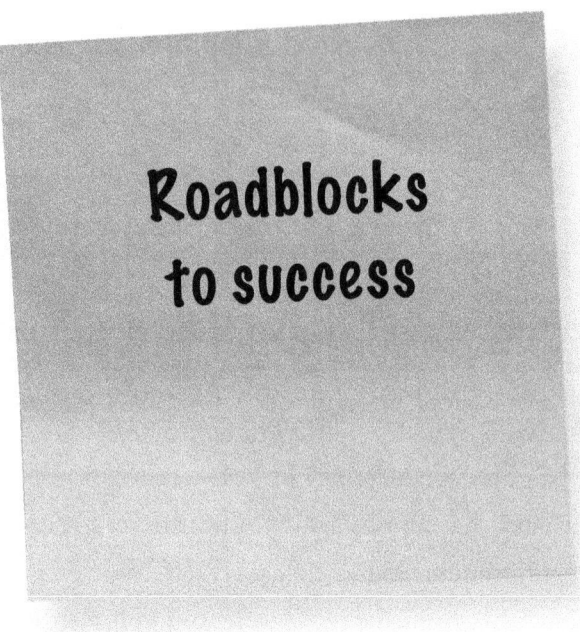

There are some fairly common roadblocks that we see businesses encounter while trying to implement CRM software. I have listed a few of them below. The good news is that each of these roadblocks is avoidable with the right planning on the front-end and the right resources to help you get off to a good start.

No strategy for lead generation, sales, and retention

In Part 1, we covered the concept of the customer lifecycle. It is so important to evaluate what you are doing in each of these areas – whether good or not so good. It's through this evaluation that you can then identify what needs to be improved and ultimately implement a strategy to handle each of these. You must know what and how you need to do things for your specific business in order to know how best to set up your CRM system. It is this system that will support the execution of your strategy.

Lack of commitment across the business

After you have identified your strategy in these key areas, the next step is to ensure that everyone in your business or team understands the strategy and agrees to make the commitment to implement and utilize CRM to help execute it.

All too often we see a specific group within a company (usually the sales/marketing team) get set up and start using the CRM software while the rest of the organization never ends up using the system.

We believe this happens for one of two reasons. It may be budgetary: The business doesn't feel it can afford to implement the software companywide. Other times there was never a "big-picture" view of the necessity and ultimate synergies achieved when a business uses the system to share information in real time across the entire team.

Consider that the system is designed to help you manage the entire customer lifecycle, including every phase of that relationship and using resources from every area of your business. Why then would you exclude anyone from having access to this system that is so foundational to managing the entire lifecycle?

This would be like giving only part of your football team a copy of the new playbook because you feel that it costs too much to print each one up. Instead, you hope that through some miracle of osmosis they will know the plays at game time. The results are predictable – whether for a sports team, or for your firm. At best, your customers will notice that you lack good form. At worst, you will lose them, and a source of your livelihood, forever.

Bottom line: Your business will never realize the full potential and impact of CRM until and unless you get the entire team utilizing the same platform.

Resistance to adoption by some users

Let's say you realize the value and necessity of including all team members in the new system. You have made plans to purchase all the necessary licenses in order to get started with this new and exciting level of organization you are about to implement in your business.

As you implement the CRM solution that you have chosen, it's important to realize that there is a critical period at the very beginning where you have to really work to ensure that you get everyone up and running and off to a good start with the system. A bad experience or lack of training can cause some users to give up or resist adopting this new platform – which can sabotage all your hard work and planning.

We can all be creatures of habit and it is often old habits that we are talking about changing to make way for a new and more effective way of doing things. If you go into the implementation process with the expectation of having to break some habits, you will be prepared to handle resistance as it comes up.

Bottom line: Good communication on the overall strategy for the company and why the CRM software is an important part of that strategy will go a long ways to mitigating resistance to change.

Lack of proper training

To further ensure successful adoption, follow up on good communication with some good training to give all users the tools they will need for a quick start.

The key is to have a good "quick start" training program in place – nothing too complex here. You should be able to train any person over the course of one to no more than three hours. If the system requires complex and lengthy training, then you should consider whether this platform is the right choice for you.

For successful training and implementation, everyone involved must have a base level of training on the system. This does a few good things for you: It allows you to set expectations for how you want the system to be used, ensuring a much more consistent approach companywide. And it ensures they really know how to use this important tool in the best way possible for your business to fully benefit.

Bottom line: There are usually multiple ways to use software to handle any given task or workflow. But there is usually only one "best practice" for a given situation and your company's specific needs.

Determine your best practices and make sure everyone on your team knows what they are.

Training across the entire team will provide you with the opportunity to properly articulate and demonstrate the best practice that you want everyone to follow when using the system.

Don't skip the most important step

CRM software is a core tool for any business, but it merely enables you to execute and deliver on a strategy that you must identify before starting. The implementation of the right software program is the easy part. The hard part here is the front-end planning needed before even deciding on the software.

If you allow yourself to fall into the trap of so many small businesses and skip this most important phase of planning, you can easily reduce a very capable CRM program to an expensive Rolodex. Without a clear plan, you may never develop a clear idea of how you can best use CRM (or any software, for that matter) in your business.

You wouldn't (or at least shouldn't) start a business without first creating a business plan. Likewise, don't run out and invest in your next CRM system before you have a clear vision of how it can best be implemented in your business.

> *"Failures don't plan to fail; they fail to plan."*
>
> *—Harvey Mackay*

Congratulations! If you have read this far, you are well on your way to making significant improvements in the way you manage the customer lifecycle in your business. It's time to put the details of your plan on paper so you have them at your fingertips.

Planning is essential as you begin the process of reviewing and ultimately deciding upon the technology you will use to execute your plan to improve the way you do business.

I see all too many cases where organizations fail to properly plan, resulting in significant struggles and a general failure to realize the results they were hoping for. Many struggle to simply tread water, while others grow swiftly and successfully through proper planning.

A good review of how your organization handles each phase of the customer lifecycle will help you develop a vision of where you want to be and what you will need to do to get there. You then can rally everyone behind that vision, making it much more likely that you will turn your goals into reality.

Our website, www.bigcontacts.com/crm-business-plan, includes a detailed business plan template that will guide you on your first steps toward improving how you do business. If you want to convert more prospects to customers and retain more of the customers you already have, it is important to build this plan in the context of the customer lifecycle. I encourage you to go to the site and download the business plan template before you begin this next section. It's best to read through the outline below and fill in your business plan as you go. This approach will ensure you can move through to completion of your CRM business plan in as little time as possible.

On the following pages is an outline of the essential components of such a plan so you can get a sense of what you need to consider and review. I introduced many of these considerations earlier; here, I am detailing them in template form to help you begin developing your business plan and to walk you through the information you will need to gather.

Your outline for action:

Finding prospects

Converting prospects to customers

Keeping your customers

General operations

I. Evaluate your <u>Lead Generation</u> process

- Create a profile of your ideal customer
- Create a list of your best and worst customers
- Evaluate the traits of your best customers

- Evaluate the traits of your worst customers
- Rank the best customers by profitability
- Find common traits among your top 5 customers

II. Identify your target market(s)

- From the profile above, you can now evaluate where your target market(s) exist. This will help you work smarter in your efforts to find and attract quality prospects.

III. Outline the needs of this target market

- This will help you to shape your messaging to ensure that you are conveying a value proposition that best resonates with your target audience. This is essential for maximizing the conversion of qualified prospects.

IV. Develop the content of your message

- Create a core body of content that will effectively deliver your value proposition (articles, blog posts, e-books, white papers, etc.) that you will use across multiple media as you work your lead generation plan.

V. Outline your multi-pronged marketing plan

- What and where will you work to get your message to your targeted audience?

- The best approach to any lead generation program is a multi-pronged one. You can't survive on a single marketing medium, so the more approaches you employ; the more consistent you will be at generating new leads for your business.

VI. Set goals so you can measure your success

- How many leads are you trying to generate per week, month, quarter, year?

- What new revenue goals are you to trying to achieve from your lead generation program over the given period?

VII. Identify the system/ database you will use to track and manage the leads that you generate.

- You will need to have a foolproof system for capturing and organizing all of these leads. The more leads you generate, the easier it is for leads to fall through the cracks.

I must admit I am a bit biased, but I have yet to find an alternative that will outperform CRM software in this area.

The answer as to which CRM software provider can best meet your needs will become apparent after you have completed your business plan and a thorough review of two or three vendors.

VIII. How will you handle leads who are not ready to buy today?

- Every lead generation program, no matter how targeted it might be, will generate a number of good leads who aren't ready to act today but are worth a continuing relationship.

- What system (if any) do you have in place to nurture leads? How do you then determine when they are ready to be handed off to a sales rep?

Coverting Prospects to Customers

I. **Evaluate your Sales Process. How do you currently handle <u>Lead Tracking</u>?**

- What system (if any) do you have in place to track your prospects? Outline your tracking and follow-up system, and decide what's working and what needs improvement.

II. What process do you have for <u>Lead Conversion</u>?

- Identify your touch points. What they are, through what medium they are delivered, what's working and what is not?

- Identify your process for qualifying and ultimately converting prospects, including the following elements:

Questioning

Identify and outline the specific line of questioning you use to ensure that you are consistently gathering the information you need to identify quality prospects.

Presenting

It's important to evaluate your current mode of presenting and the overall level of content that you are presenting to your prospects.

Determine the best mix and flow of content you will typically present to a prospect. The key here is to briefly review their pain points, provide the right amount of education on your product or service, effectively present your value proposition, and give them a compelling reason(s) to move forward to closure.

Handling objections

Identify and list all objections that you commonly hear when dealing with your prospects. After you have created an exhaustive list of these objections, you will want to write out at least two or three rebuttals for each.

After you write them out, read through them, role play with them and ultimately fine-tune them to a point where you are comfortable that they will hold up in a real world sales scenario. You want to feel confident that a sales rep can use these with a prospect and come across in a credible and convincing manner to defuse the concern and keep the sales process moving forward.

Closing

If you were able to ask good questions, really listen to the answers, present information in a way that resonated, and handle objections with solid answers, you have likely already won the business.

A well-orchestrated sales process that meets a prospect's needs during their buying process can help make their decision to purchase the logical next step.

This is the ideal scenario, but often prospects still need a guiding hand and a few well-placed closing questions to nudge them into their new status as "customer."

It is important to develop a list of compelling closing questions. These should preserve your image as a "consultant" and not a high-pressure salesperson, but the questions nonetheless need to be somewhat pointed.

If you have done everything right to this point and feel confident that your selling process has matched their buying process and your solution truly meets their needs, then you should be confident in asking some good closing questions.

As you work through this section of the plan, you will want to consider this checklist of questions. Answers to these questions will help you pinpoint what needs to be done to make lasting improvements.

- What areas need improvement or have issues?

- Where there are issues, what is causing them?

- What needs to be improved in your sales process?

- Can you outline specific stages in your sales pipeline?

- Which stages need improvement or have issues?

- What is causing the issues in those stages?

- Do any stages need to be added or removed from your pipeline?

I. Evaluate your <u>Customer Retention Process</u>

- After the initial sale has been made, what are you doing to stay top of mind with your existing clients so that they think of you next time they are ready to purchase a product or service that you offer?

- If you offer multiple products and services, what are you doing to stay in touch to work on cross-selling and up-selling where appropriate?

II. Identify the area(s) of your business that <u>influence customer retention</u>

- Customer service
- Technical support
- Client communication
- Other?

III. Identify what each area is currently doing to <u>improve client retention</u>

- What activities are helping you to service, support, and retain customers? As you identify these activities, separate them into two buckets
- Activities that are working well
- Activities that need improvement

IV. Where there are issues, <u>identify what's causing them</u>

V. Identify your current <u>customer and prospect touch-points</u>

- How do you typically contact and communicate with your customers? (phone, letter, email)

- For each of these common touch points, identify common scripts for calls or text for letters and templates.

- Create a polished version of each communication and label them to know when and where to use them in your process.

This text can then be used as templates to streamline your processes going forward.

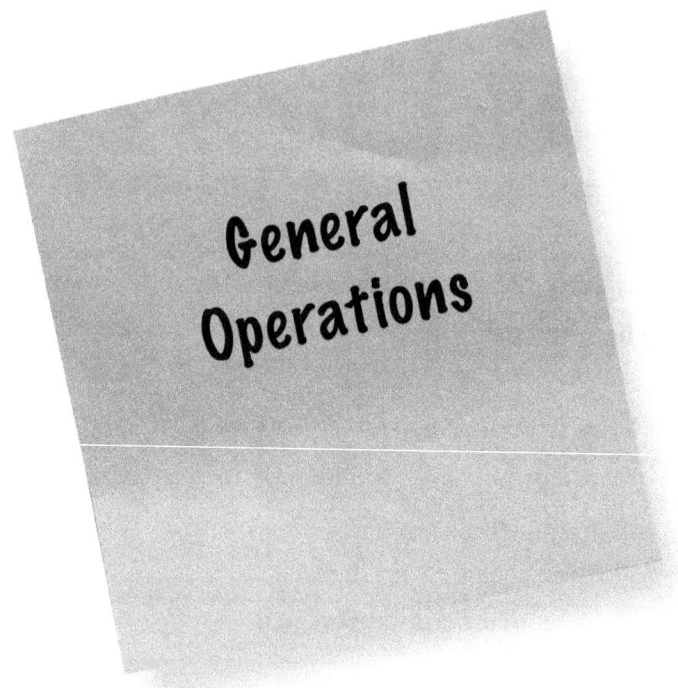

I. Evaluate your workflow processes

- One of the best ways to get more operationally efficient and develop a consistent approach that will keep customers happy is to identify a list of workflows and steps in each workflow.

- These workflows are the activities you perform on a continuing basis to meet the needs of your prospects and customers throughout the lifecycle.

- A good CRM system will have a customizable workflow management module that allows you to bundle and manage a series of tasks to create seamless and repeatable processes within your business.

- A workflow management module will allow you to define different workflows for various types of jobs or processes. At each stage in the workflow, one individual or group is responsible for a specific task.

- Once the task is complete, the workflow module ensures that the individuals responsible for the next task are notified and receive the data they need to execute their stage of the process.

- All of this works to ensure that things don't fall through the cracks, and it will greatly help you increase the amount of business you can handle without having to hire additional employees.

- There is an entire industry dedicated to workflow management or Business Process Management (BPM), and there are many software programs dedicated to this. The key thing to know here is that there is really no need for a small business to invest in a separate and potentially expensive workflow management system.

- You can realize many of the benefits and efficiencies from a good CRM system that goes beyond single-step tasks and allows you to create multi-step workflows. Finally, you will want to make sure it also allows you to assign different steps to different members of your team or business.

II. Identify the workflows that your business performs on an ongoing basis

- Include the name of the workflow, the tasks (steps) involved, and who is responsible for each task.

- From this listing of workflows you can then begin to identify what processes are working well and what needs improvement. You can also identify what might be missing and needs to be added to better serve your customers throughout their entire lifecycle.

The end goal here is that you will ultimately be able to load these workflows/ processes into a system (CRM software) to begin tracking what you are doing for who and when. You will then be able to determine if you are really delivering on the promises you are making to your prospects and customers.

- As mentioned earlier, you can't evaluate and improve what you can't measure. This operational aspect of your business is very important to define and then track over time. This is where the rubber meets the road in terms of improving customer retention for your business.

III. Identify workflows that are improving efficiency

IV. Identify workflows that need improvement or are causing issues

- Where there are issues, identify what's causing them.

V. Identify workflows that need to be added to your processes

- By identifying all that you do well today and how you can improve on other processes, you will be in better shape than 90 percent of the businesses out there.

VI. Determine how you want to <u>share information within your company</u>

- Most Web-based CRM software platforms are by default an "open platform" where all information is available and can be shared by all team members. This type of structure may be just what you need.

- On the other hand there may be some types of reports and even certain contacts to which you wish to restrict access. You may even have certain employees who are part time or seasonal and you wish to restrict what they can do in the system. You may want to limit what they can view and allow them to only add information, not delete it.

- The various levels of permissions you might want to grant to various employees within your company could involve as many as four or five levels of access that could include owner(s), manager(s), administrator(s), and general employee(s).

One the biggest challenges, and potentially biggest rewards, in setting up a CRM system relates to how you organize and categorize your database of contacts. Often companies simply import their contact list and jump right in with the same organization (or lack thereof) that they had before.

The good news is that many have upgraded from programs that are more like basic address books to a full-featured CRM system. This alone will pay huge dividends for them.

The bad news is that many do not invest a little time on the front end to think through how their contacts are currently organized and how they could be better organized.

As you think through this aspect of your database, consider how you want to group your contacts to easily pull targeted lists to perform key functions in your business. Whether you need to pull a list of customers to follow up on an event you have coming up, want to send a marketing email to your current prospects, announce a new product to your existing customers, or engage in any sort of communication with your prospects and customers, you will need an easy way to identify each of these targeted groups.

At the end of the day if you organize your contacts in a way that best suits the goals and needs of your business, you will be much more effective at taking a mountain of contacts and quickly pulling out meaningful subsections that you can work on at a given time. All of this effort on the front end will prevent customers and prospects from falling off the radar.

Finally, all of this organization will allow you to effectively handle more customers and prospects without the need for more people and overhead. This efficiency will ultimately lead to happier clients, lower operating expenses and increased sales.

Let's start with the end in mind for a different perspective. Think about your day-to-day business and all the things you need to do to run it. Now imagine for a moment that you are perfectly organized and can put your fingers on any information as you need it.

Make a list of information you might need to access regarding your customers and prospects. It might be that you need to generate a list of the prospects you met at the trade show last week to send them a quick email. Maybe you want to see the most current status of your sales pipeline to get a handle on where you are for the month. Or imagine you finally have a long-awaited product or feature and want to generate a list of all customers and prospects who have expressed an interest in it.

You get the idea here. The more complete this list is and the clearer you are about what you would want to be able to see in each situation, the easier it will be for you to then work backward to determine how to organize and label your contacts to achieve those results.

A good CRM system should offer at least three or four field types for organizing your contacts and allow you to customize each. Below are what I consider the "core four" that you should require in your next CRM system.

1. Contact Types

Look at this field as the "30,000-foot view" of your contacts. They are the very general categories you create within your system. (Prospects, Clients, Vendors, Family, Personal, etc.) These are usually organized into a "pick list" or a series of "radio buttons" to choose from. Think of this as the very first layer of segmenting your contacts. As we move into each of the other methods below, we are able to get more granular in how we parse and sort our contacts. Because this is designed to identify your general types of contacts, I suggest no more than six to eight types.

2. Groups & Categories

Moving down to about a "15,000-foot view," you will want the flexibility to customize and build a handful of groups and categories within your system. Here you would track things such as industry, region, and referral source. The typical format of this type of custom field is a "pick list." The key factor in determining when you use this is simple. If you have very specific and finite values that you want someone to select from, then you will load them here. You determine what you want to call or label each group or category, load all of the options you want someone to be able to choose from, and you're done. This method prevents anyone from entering his or her own "version" of the information and will ensure that your data stays "clean" and accurate when you pull reports later.

For example, if you and I were both to identify what industry a client is in, I might type "Financial" and you might type "Financial Services." The pick list allows you to set the standard label and prevent any deviation. Anything overdone can become a hindrance. We suggest that this sort of organization be contained to no more than five or six groups or categories. Remember, we are still flying at a high level here. There is a more granular method called "Tags" that we will cover in a moment.

3. Custom Fields

We're still flying at about 15,000 feet. The difference here is that you may want to create fields without knowing exactly the options you'll have. A custom field is free-form, allowing users to type in exactly what they need. You still create the label for the field, but the data entered is up to the individual. The most effective use of custom fields usually involves no more than 8-10 different values.

4. Tags

Finally, we have "Tags." This relatively new and unique method has really opened the door for creating multiple associations and labels for a given contact. This is your most granular level of categorization within the database. It allows you the flexibility to assign multiple values/categories to a single contact. For example, you might want to track someone's interests (golf, tennis, wine, etc.), and you want to easily keep track of products that they have an interest in or products that you have already sold to them. If you think of all the possible subsets for labeling a particular contact, it could get very cumbersome to create a custom field or pick list to accommodate all your needs. Tags are a very quick and easy way to create a label and apply it to any one of a number of contacts. As your business evolves and as products, interests, and campaigns change, it is easy to replace labels.

Begin to visualize what your contact list would look like if you were to sort it into natural groups and categories. Consider a few basic questions:

How many groups or categories do you need to be able to divide your customers and prospects into effectively manage them?

How would you label each group?

Are there subgroups or categories you need to track within broader groups and categories?

Do you have contacts that you would like to associate with more than one group?

We encourage our customers to open a Word document, a spreadsheet, or simply take out a sheet of paper to begin identifying the various groups, interests, categories and general opportunities that exist within their current list of contacts.

I have seen countless examples of this approach and I can tell you that this exercise will produce big dividends for you over time. A well-organized database of contacts can help you to:

- Build stronger customer relationships.
- Increase your sales.
- Create a more efficient business.

Now that you have a basic understanding of the four primary categorization fields, it's time to take out that worksheet and get busy. I have a template worksheet that works great for this exercise. You can download it at www.bigcontacts.com/crm-business-plan.

As you work through this, it is important to know that there are two dimensions to the whole process.

1. Identifying and outlining the overall categorization/ grouping of your contacts. This is the part where you write down all of the names and labels for each of these fields.

2. Identifying the type of field you will need to properly house and display that custom data.

Here are some good questions to ask for each custom label you identify to determine what field type you will want to use.

- Is this a set value that will best be selected from a pick list in order to save time with data entry and ensure consistency in how this value is entered for the contact? If this is the case, then you may want to consider using a pick list or drop-down list field to house this information.

- Is this a value that needs to be free-form to allow for flexibility in what is actually entered here? If this is the case, then you will want a basic custom field here that allows for free-form text entry.

- Is this field one that may require more than one associated or related value? If this is the case then you will want to either use a pick list that allows for multiple selections at one time, or better yet you, may want to use Tags as this is typically the most efficient way to assign multiple related values to a single contact.

If you invest the time on the front end to outline your needs and use elements of all these methods, your CRM system is sure to become a more powerful tool in managing your customer and prospect relationships.

Choose the contact record format

When evaluating CRM software for your small business, it is important to understand the difference between a Contact Centric system and an Account (Business) Centric system.

Choosing incorrectly is one of the biggest mistakes that you could make when selecting a CRM system, as most only offer one format or the other. You want to make certain that the system you choose will format and display the contact record in the manner you need for your business.

At BigContacts, we give you that choice. This allows our customers to start one way and change their minds later. I believe that this sort of flexibility is required when dealing with some of your most important data.

In Contact Centric systems, the primary organization is centered on the individual contact. In Account (Business) Centric systems, there are two levels to the basic organization: a "Business" (or account) layer to which multiple individual contacts can be related or linked.

If you're working in an industry where you only need one contact record per account or primarily work with individuals, you may want the simplicity of Contact Centric option. However, if you need to track multiple contacts per account (business) then the Account (Business) Centric becomes the best option. Below is each option, explained in a bit more detail.

Contact Centric Format

In a Contact Centric system, the database is organized around individual contacts. So, let's say it might be typical that you have dealings with multiple people all from the same company. If you were to use the Contact Centric format, you would have several different (completely separate) contact records, and in each record you would see the company name. There is no way to pull these separate records into a single view to get a more global view of the communications and activity that is going on with this company as a whole. This format is fine as long as you have no need for the consolidated view of all activity that then allows you to drill down into each of the individual contacts as needed.

A Contact Centric organization makes more sense if you typically deal with individuals or a single point of contact when dealing with a company. This format can become very difficult and clumsy when trying to track communication with multiple individuals at a particular company. It can also be a challenge if you have a need to track company level information separate from the individuals you are dealing with at that company.

For example, you may want to track information about the company (e.g. sic code, # employees, annual budget, etc.) separately from individual contact information (e.g. favorite hobby, home phone number, spouse's name, etc.).

There really isn't an easy way to do this. Under which contact do you store the company information? Which contact becomes the primary record? Do you store the information under both contacts... which makes updating information even more difficult? Do you create a "contact" record to serve as the company record and somehow relate the contacts to it?

Account (Business) Centric Format

Account (Business) Centric systems have a layer above the individual contact – the "account" or "business" that allows you to link multiple "individual" contacts under that business. This can offer several advantages, including the ability to track company-related information entirely separate from contact-related information. This approach also makes it easier to:

- See all opportunities for an account/company
- See combined history for all contacts at that company
- See the company and all contacts in a single view
- Generate reports on both company and individuals

Prepare your database for import

Now that you have completed your CRM business plan and know how you want to organize your new database, it's time to prepare the information you will be importing so that it maps into your new organization.

Depending on the environment you are coming from, you will need to get your data in shape so you can start with a "clean" database. You will want to clean up your database before you import it.

Contact data can get pretty messy over time if it has not been periodically purged of duplicate or old information. This should be an ongoing management process, but often that doesn't get done. Don't get me wrong: I'm not saying your database has to be perfect before you import it, but there are some basics that should come first.

Armed with your detailed business plan and with a clear picture of what you will need to accommodate it, now's the time to go shopping. It's time to find the CRM system that will work best for your company.

Part III

Choosing the right CRM software for your business

"It's not hard to make decisions when you know what your values are."

-Roy Disney

When conducting any review, it is important to know the questions to ask and to have a system for comparing apples to apples as best you can. CRM software has so many features and dimensions to it that it is more important than ever that you take a systematic approach to this process. This is the only way to ensure you find the best fit for your company.

If you look at that review on two levels, you can better evaluate and rank your options. There is the provider level, and the product level. There are certain things you want to look for and demand that the provider offer. There will be features the product will need for your specific needs.

As you answer the following questions on what each of the solutions offers, you will want to rank them. Included on our site at www.bigcontacts.com/crm-business-plan you will find a worksheet for this evaluation.

Provider Level Criteria

1. **Customer self-service** – Are there resources available that make it easy for you to locate answers to your questions 24/7?

2. **Help functionality** – You want a help/support suite that is intuitive yet comprehensive. You should be able to find answers to virtually any question you may have about the software.

3. **Support** – As referenced earlier, a good level of support should be included with the price of the software, including email ticketing support and live chat. It's good to pay attention to how responsive a vendor is during your selection. Keep in mind that you are buying more than just the software – you're also buying the service and support that the vendor will deliver. If you're uncom-

fortable with the service or support, then don't invest in the software.

Training –Training videos should be available so that you can learn at your own pace, and the company should at least offer live training to you and your team even if it is for an additional charge. There may be situations that are specific to your business and you will need answers that a generic video cannot deliver.

1. **Intuitiveness of system** – The system should be so easy to use that anyone on your team can jump right in and start using it. A good system should require very little training to get started.

2. **System navigation** – Really pay attention to how many clicks and tabs (on average) it takes for key functions. These are the things that you will be using day in and day out to manage your prospect and customer relationships. It may not seem like a big deal at first, but over time the number of clicks and tabs you must navigate to perform your key tasks each day can have an impact on how much you can get done and the ground you can cover in a day.

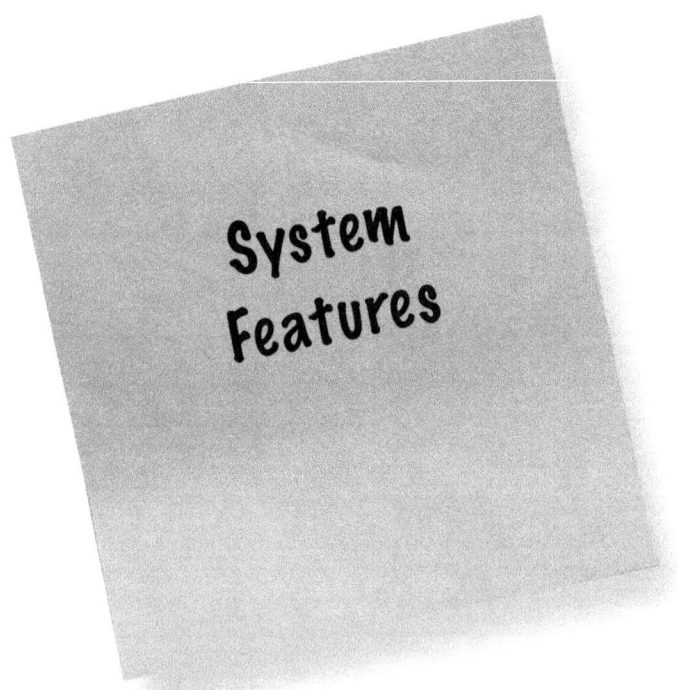

When evaluating any system, it helps to look at it from the perspective of the customer lifecycle, which encompasses the essence of managing and growing your business:

FIND the right prospects

What tools / modules does the system offer to help you more effectively:

- Capture and organize leads from your website.

- Nurture leads through automated email marketing.

CONVERT more Prospects to Customers

What tools/ modules does the system offer to help you more effectively:

- Capture and record key information about your prospects and their needs and priorities.

- Track opportunities through each stage of your sales process.

- Deliver ongoing drip marketing campaigns as needed throughout the sales process – ensuring that you stay top of mind to your prospects as they move through their buying process.

- Provide automated tasks / reminders to your sales people to ensure that they touch base with the prospect at the right times throughout the sales process – ensuring that no opportunity falls through the cracks.

KEEP more customers

What tools / modules does the system offer to help you more effectively:

- Touch base on a regular schedule with your customers – providing product updates, delivering educational information, special offers, etc. All this designed to do two things:
  - Stay top of mind with your customers so that next time they go to make a purchase they will think of you.

  - To remind them that you care about them and appreciate their business.

- Manage your workflows and tasks to ensure timely customer service and follow-up.

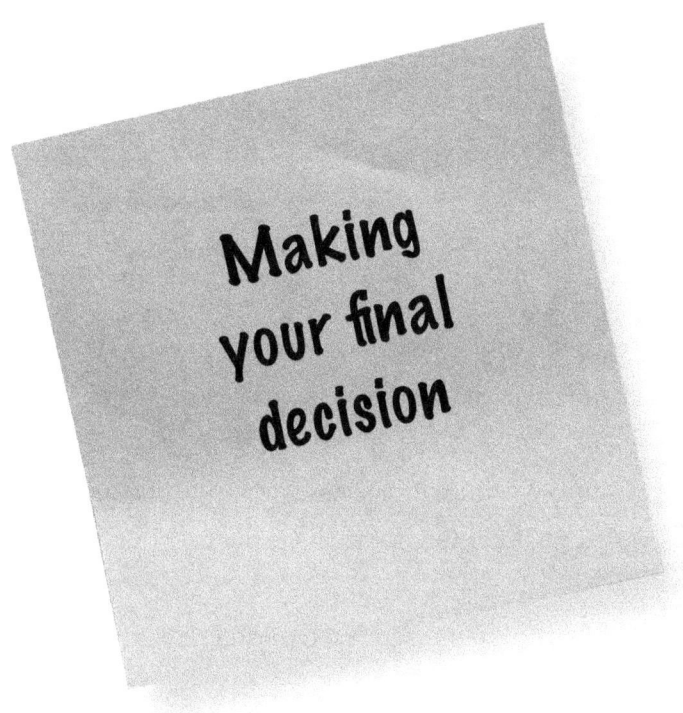

After you have completed your review and ranking of systems, you now have a thorough side-by-side comparison to make your most informed decision. Take this comparison you have created, review it, and create your short list. By this time you should be looking at your top 2 picks.

It's time for another look over these options, and one way to make your decision (especially if they are all looking the same at this point) is to use the tried and true "Ben Franklin Method." Franklin essentially invented the "T Chart," and this is a great tool to use here.

Every decision has its advantages and disadvantages. The challenge is to figure out which choice will provide you with the greatest net advantage based on your priorities and specific needs.

The Ben Franklin T Chart will help you to make a good choice by allowing you to:

- Identify the important elements you will use to make your decision

- Rank the importance of each element (1-10) to determine which have a greater weighting in your decision

- Grade the choices you have in front of you (1-10) in relation to each of these elements

- Multiply the importance factor by the ranking to come up with a total number for each element

- Add up the columns for each option to come up with the winner

It's from this very methodical approach that you can easily "break the tie" between two choices. Adding up each of their total scores will clearly determine the choice that will in fact deliver the greatest net benefit to you over the long run.

Your top two choices are likely very close in what they can do, but neither is going to be perfect, so I encourage you to use the Ben Franklin T-Chart provided on our website at www.bigcontacts.com/crm-business-plan and fill it out for each of your top choices. I have included some guidance for you on the worksheet so that you can do it like Ben did and make a great decision.

After you have completed the T Chart, I think it should be fairly obvious whom you will choose for the CRM software for your business.

The key to a successful CRM investment is basing your decision on a careful definition of your requirements. These requirements are derived from the pain or problems you are currently experiencing and the functionality required to solve these issues.

The technology or "bells and whistles" are only part of the CRM equation. If you undertake the CRM selection process before you have figured out how CRM aligns with your objectives, and how it will affect and enhance your processes, you are only increasing the likelihood of facing some real challenges as you implement the software.

Avoid taking this "bottom-up" approach of looking at particular capabilities and technology first. The risks far outweigh any rewards. For one, we have seen many companies end up spending a lot of money on low-benefit capabilities. Instead, I encourage you to opt for the more effective and more rewarding top-down "requirements-driven" approach.

After you are comfortable that you have a clear handle on all of your key requirements, it's time to take a test drive. It's likely that you wouldn't buy a car without one. Neither should you make a decision about software that will help you drive your business without taking a test drive.

Any vendor you are considering should offer you a thirty-day free trial of the software. You would think that one free trial is the same as any other, but this is not always the case. There are a few important questions to ask about the free trial to ensure that you will be able to get a true sense of how well the company's CRM software will function within your business.

- Will they allow you to add all of the users you will need for your company during this trial?

This is important, as this is really the only way to accurately see the benefits of having your entire team on the system, sharing information in real time and managing workflow, etc., across your company.

- Do they give you access to all the features/ modules during the trial? If not, why?

This too is very important, as it is really the only way to ensure you are able to experience all capabilities. Verifying that the functionality exists is one thing, but discovering how the product actually offers the functionality it claims to have is another.

At BigContacts we offer both of the above, plus we give our free trial users a bonus. Often the only way to get a true sense of the system is to use it as if it were already yours. This can mean that you have already invested a good bit of time customizing fields and entering real customer data.

When you upgrade one of our free-trial accounts to a paid edition, all of that time you have invested is not lost. We retain all of the customization and all information that you have entered. After you upgrade to a paid account, you can simply pick up where you left off during the free trial period.

The journey to where you have arrived may seem long, but I can assure you that the work you have just completed will pay dividends for you and your business for years to come. You now have all the ingredients to take your business to the next level. It's time to push this project to a successful completion.

Successfully implementing this software is really now a result of all that has been defined in your business plan.

One of the best approaches is to create a timeline. A timeline has a few important benefits for you:

- It ensures that you have all the implementation steps clearly outlined so you know what to do and when.

- It forces you to find and block time in your schedule to oversee the implementation.

- It ensures that you don't move too fast and take any shortcuts as you are about to finish this important phase.

I have included a template that I highly recommend you use to help create your own timeline. This template can be downloaded at www.bigcontacts.com/crm-business-plan.

Your timeline and implementation should flow like this:

1. Review your completed business plan

This will be your roadmap as you work through the customization and overall setup of the software. You will want to review this with anyone helping you in this process and keep it handy to be able to refer back to it often.

2. Customize your system

With the business plan in hand, you will want to go in and begin customizing each area of your system as needed. Depending on your needs and how easy the system is to customize, this step can involve some time to implement. This will be one of the largest segments of your implementation timeline but will also be one that produces the largest benefit over the long run.

A system that is easy to customize can be set up in-house by you or one of your coworkers. If the system you chose is more involved, you may need to have this work done by the vendor. There will likely be a charge for this work, and hopefully the company shared with you, early on, its rates for custom work.

3. Prepare your current database for import

As mentioned in Chapter 7, it really depends on where you are coming from as to how much you have to do to get your data in shape so you start with a "clean" database. Clean up your database before you import.

There are some basic things you will want to do before importing your database.

- Eliminate duplicate contacts if possible.

- Remove (noncustomer) contacts that you currently have no intention of trying to convert to customers. You can always add a list when you are ready to work with them. Otherwise you are just creating unnecessary clutter in your system.

- After you have done this and now have a fairly clean list of your contacts, you will want to export them to an Excel spreadsheet (just prior to import) and add the necessary columns to accommodate any new custom fields you have created.

After you add the column, you will then label the column header with the name of this custom field. Finally, you will add the custom data for each contact as appropriate and as known. Adding a new column for this custom data and loading the values where you can, will save you countless hours after import. This method allows you to get all custom data loaded at one time when it is imported.

4. Import your data

The type of system and the level of information you are currently tracking for your prospects will also dictate the level and type of data import that is needed to get your customer and prospect data properly imported into this new system.

In general, there are three levels of complexity in the system you may already have today. They are each listed below along with the general type of import that is required to ensure that all of your data is properly transferred.

- No system – We often find that companies that are currently not using a CRM system are tracking their customer and prospect information using Excel spread sheets. It's likely that they have the contact's name, address, phone and email address in the spreadsheet. There may also be some basic notes about each contact.

The spreadsheet method is very time-consuming and cumbersome to update with each interaction, so we often find little more than this core contact information.

If that's your scenario, then you should be able to import your data into your new CRM system using a self-serve "import wizard" offered by the software vendor. Hopefully, you have already determined what import tools they offer, and what if any costs are associated with using them, prior to making your purchase. This will ensure there are no surprises regarding your setup costs.

- Address book – This is one step up the contact management food chain. Depending on the system you are using there may be some additional information that you can track about your contacts.

The good part of this type of system vs. a spreadsheet is that the fields are labeled for you. You're not creating your database from scratch. The information you are able to collect is still very basic and what we consider "core" contact information.

Any system (or spreadsheet) that contains this "core" contact information and does not contain a full contact history (all the stuff you find in an actual CRM system – notes, meetings, task, emails, etc.) will require a very simple import. Most systems on the market today allow you to use what is often referred to as an "import wizard." This tool should be a standard and you should be able to use it for free to import all your core contact information (along with any additional information that will reside in your custom fields).

- CRM system – If you have already been using a CRM system of some sort then you have developed a "contact history" over time for each of your prospects and customers (notes, meetings, tasks, emails, etc.) You will want to import all of this information, but the wizard will likely not be able to handle that.

An import from one CRM system to another requires the help of a qualified technician with direct access to the back end of the database. This "custom import" will often involve a fee as there can be a considerable amount of a technician's time and some back and forth between you and your new vendor to ensure that all data is mapped correctly and organized properly. Again, this is something that your vendor has likely already quoted to you. Hopefully, there are no surprises for you at this late stage.

The system is now customized with the fields you need to effectively handle your prospects and customers; the data from your old system is now cleaned up, imported and neatly organized in your new system. Time to relax…

Not quite. But we're almost there.

The very last thing you should do before you head off to that much-needed vacation is to ensure that you have a training schedule.

5. Roll out an organized training schedule

As mentioned earlier, the first thirty days after installing anything new (including CRM software) is a critical period. You must ensure that you get everyone off to a good start.

As mentioned previously, a bad experience or lack of training can cause some users to give up or resist adopting the new platform – which can sabotage all your hard work.

As creatures of habit, we often require a little hand-holding to ensure we can break those old habits and move on to a better way of doing things. The key to combating this issue is to have a good "quick-start" training program in place.

I have found that the most successful implementations require everyone to have a base level of training on the system. The training will allow you to set expectations for how you want the system to be used – ensuring a much more consistent approach across your entire company.

Welcome to a new world with the right CRM software now part of your business. You will find over time that CRM is more than just software. It is also about business strategy.

CRM will help you to better understand, anticipate and respond to the needs of your customers and prospects.

I hope the time you invested in reading this book will save you countless headaches and help you to generate more revenue over the long run.

We've covered a lot of ground, so let me put everything in perspective as I wrap up. The summary below should serve as a quick reference for you in the future. You may want to revisit this book months down the road, and you can turn to this section to review the main takeaways and how you can apply them to your business.

The lifeblood of any business is the customer. Without customers, a business has nothing, regardless of the product or service that you offer. Today your customers have access to so much information that it is easy for your business to become just another commodity.

Without customers a business has nothing,
regardless of the product or service that you offer.

To grow your business in a competitive landscape, you must be able to effectively find, convert and keep as many new customers as possible. To ensure your long-term success, you must master each of the three phases of the "customer lifecycle."

Doing so requires a thorough review of each phase to identify where you are and what you need to do to strengthen your processes. This will help ensure a smooth and consistent flow of new customers and a growing base of existing loyal customers.

Master the customer lifecycle and maximize profits.

Getting a handle on all phases of the customer lifecycle will help you to convert more prospects to customers and keep more of those you have.

After you have identified all that needs to be done in each phase, it's time to execute! There is no better tool than CRM software to get your arms around this entire lifecycle.

The customer is the central theme in this book, and the "C" in CRM (Customer Relationship Management) is all about the customer. With the right match, CRM software will help you organize and grow your business. The key phrase here is the "right match."

It is very important that you follow an organized process to identify your specific needs so that you know what to look for and ultimately make the right choice for your CRM software.

CRM software will help you

get your arms around managing the entire customer lifecycle.
This software is the single best tool for the job and will help you
leverage available information to establish and strengthen your
customer relationships.

As you review your business processes and evaluate what you
are doing in each phase of the lifecycle, get all of this information
on paper and create your CRM business plan. Organizing your
thoughts and putting them on paper will help you to make the best
decision when choosing such a foundational tool for your business.
The solution for mastering the customer lifecycle is not just about
technology, per se. It's about knowing when, where, why and how to
apply technology to the mix. Your CRM business plan will help you
to answer these questions.

Create a CRM business plan

to ensure that you choose the best CRM software to meet your
needs. The business plan will help you to determine when, where,
why and how to apply technology to the customer lifecycle.

CRM software has so many features and dimensions that it is
more important than ever to systematically approach your selection.
This is the only way to ensure you find the best fit for your company.

You will want to look for certain features and services to meet your specific business needs. Make no purchase unless the provider offers them.

Choose the right CRM software for your business
by knowing what questions to ask and then comparing the answers to those questions to your specific needs.

One of the best approaches to implementing your new software is to create a timeline. This timeline will ensure that you have all the steps clearly outlined with an order of when to do what. It will also force you to find and block time in your schedule to oversee the implementation. Finally, it will ensure that you don't move too fast and take any shortcuts as you are about to finish this important phase of the whole process.

Create a timeline for implementation
to ensure your success in getting your system customized, your data organized, and your people trained. Accomplishing these three things will pay dividends for you and your business for years to come.

If you have yet to actually create your plan of action using the resources in this book, I encourage you to take the next step and get started today. It is well worth your time. Again, you will find all the worksheets for creating for plan of action at www.bigcontacts.com/crm-business-plan.

Regardless of where you are in the process today, I thank you for your interest in an area that I consider crucial to the future growth of your business.

After you complete your CRM business plan, I invite you to give BigContacts a look to see if our CRM software might meet your specific needs based on the information you have now compiled. The Web address for BigContacts is http://www.bigcontacts.com/ and, as mentioned earlier, we offer a thirty-day free trial. Here is also a direct link to the free trial: https://webapp.bigcontacts.com/signup-trial/signup.php

This trial account will allow you to add all the users you will need for your company. This is really the only way to accurately see the benefits of having your entire team on the system, sharing information in real time and managing workflow.

We also give you access to all the features and modules in your trial account. This is really the only way to ensure you are able to experience all of the capabilities of the software. Verifying that the functionality exists is one thing, but discovering how the product actually delivers the functionality it claims to have is another.

Finally, we give you another bonus. Often the only way to get a true sense of the system is to use it as if it were already yours. This can mean that you have already invested a good bit of time customizing fields and entering real customer data.

When you upgrade one of our free trial accounts to a paid edition, all of that time you have invested entering data is not lost. We retain all of the customization and all of the customer information that you have entered. After you upgrade to a paid account with us, you can simply pick up from where you left off during the free trial.

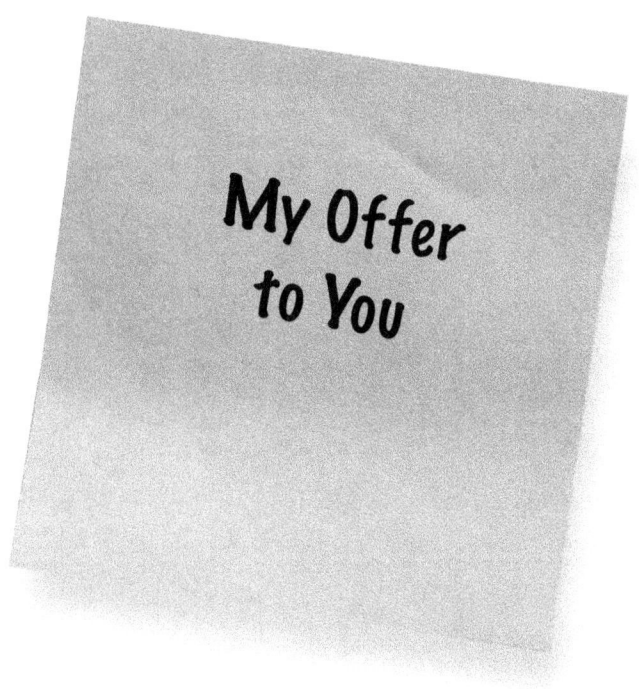

If you decide that BigContacts is the right system for you, I would like to offer you a bonus for buying this book and going through this process with me. I will give you our <u>System Setup and Customization Service package</u> – free of charge. Depending on the size and complexity of your database, this would normally cost you between $200 and $600 for the initial customization and setup.

Simply upgrade to a paid account with BigContacts, and then contact one of our customer service representatives at 1.888.286.6578. On this call you can give them the following reference number (**BC-FSCS-11**) and they will arrange for your free consultations with one of our in-house small-business advisers.

After speaking with one of our advisers, you will have all of your custom data fields in place as well as your core contact data imported and ready to use in BigContacts.

I wish you well with whatever CRM system you decide is right for your business. If you have any questions about anything you have read in this book, or CRM questions in general, you can always contact me via email at bob.walton@bigcontacts.com

You can look forward to a prosperous future as you master the customer lifecycle.

Bob Walton
Founder | CEO
BigContacts
www.bigcontacts.com